THE POLITICS OF PUBLIC LIBRARIANSHIP

Recent Titles in
New Directions in Information Management

The Politics of Public Librarianship

DAVID SHAVIT

NEW DIRECTIONS IN INFORMATION MANAGEMENT,
NUMBER 12

GREENWOOD PRESS
NEW YORK · WESTPORT, CONNECTICUT · LONDON

Library of Congress Cataloging-in-Publication Data

Shavit, David.
  The politics of public librarianship.

  (New directions in information management,
ISSN 0887–3844 ; no. 12)
  Bibliography: p.
  Includes index.
  1. Public libraries—Administration—Political
aspects—United States. 2. Libraries and state—
United States. 3. Library science—Political aspects—
United States. 4. Library administration—Decision
making. I. Title. II. Series.
Z678.S5 1986   025.1   86–7573
ISBN 0–313–24816–8 (lib. bdg. : alk. paper)

Library of Congress Catalog Card Number: 86–7573
ISBN: 0–313–24816–8
ISSN: 0887–3844

First published in 1986

Greenwood Press, Inc.
88 Post Road West, Westport, Connecticut 06881

Printed in the United States of America

The paper used in this book complies with the
Permanent Paper Standard issued by the National
Information Standards Organization (Z39.48–1984).

10 9 8 7 6 5 4 3 2 1

To the memories of my Father and Mother

Contents

Contents

Tables

Preface

"Surely it is high time to stop being frightened by a word. Politics includes the making of governmental decisions, and the effort or struggle to gain or keep the power to make those decisions."[1] Thus wrote Thomas Eliot in the first serious article on the politics of education, which led to the emergence of this new discipline. In *The Public Library in the Political Process*, published over thirty-five years ago as part of the Public Library Inquiry, Oliver Garceau wrote in the same vein:

By and large, public librarians are not thinking as employees of government or department heads in a public bureaucracy. They are nevertheless inescapably a part of government and involved in "politics." ... It is of paramount importance to librarians, to library science, and to the citizen that public librarians understand and appreciate more clearly the political world of the public library. It has been the purpose of this report to bring to the attention of librarians that public administration at every level is a political process, operating within a matrix of political forces, adjusting to and building on dynamic political change in the community.[2]

In the years since Garceau's study appeared, no new comprehensive study of this subject has been published although several books and articles dealing with specific topics have appeared. The politics of public librarianship is still a largely uncharted area of research. The fact that *Library Literature* still does not contain a subject heading on Politics and Librarianship is only one indication of this situation. While the literature on the politics of public librarianship is meager, the extensive literature on the politics of education, published since Eliot's article, has been particularly useful for this study.

This book tries to remedy this situation by providing a survey of the politics of public librarianship, the nature and impact of the political forces surrounding and influencing public librarianship, and the political characteristics of the public library. It deals with the policies of local, state, and federal governments as they relate to public librarianship and explores the political issues that affect it.

Politics refers to the struggle over public decisions that determine public policies and to the methods by which resources are allocated; it is synonymous with the governmental policy-making process. Any governmental process involving authoritative decisions on the allocation of resources is of a political nature. Public libraries are part of government; they are, therefore, political entities. Public librarianship is a political issue at the local, state, and federal levels. Library boards and library administrators are engaged in the governmental policy-making process, and are political participants in that process.

The widely held belief that public libraries are "apolitical," somehow unattached to the political structures and processes of their communities, is erroneous. The public library is a political enterprise. Politics and public libraries are interrelated. Politics occurs at various levels within public librarianship, as well as between the public library and other governmental institutions. Public librarians are realizing that public libraries are not outside the body politic, that they are not isolated from the political scene, and that politics in public librarianship is necessary. The increase in state and federal funding for public libraries and the need to lobby these levels of government has increased the interest of public librarians in state and federal political systems and in their role in the politics of public librarianship.

A research project on President Lyndon Johnson and the

National Advisory Commission on Libraries was the point of departure for this book. I wish to express my thanks to the National Endowment for the Humanities, which provided me with a travel grant to the Lyndon Johnson Library in Austin, Texas, and to the staff of the Johnson Library. I would also like to thank my research assistants Beth Nickels and Bonnie Chojnicki for their editorial help.

NOTES

1. Thomas H. Eliot, "Toward an Understanding of Public School Politics," *American Political Science Review* 52 (December 1959): 1035.

2. Oliver Garceau, *The Public Library in the Political Process* (New York: Columbia University Press, 1949), p. 239.

THE POLITICS OF PUBLIC LIBRARIANSHIP

1

The Myth of Apolitical Public Librarianship

Preconceived notions, ideologies, and values have marked the politics of American public librarianship. Public librarianship has been functioning under the myth that public libraries are not political institutions.

The myth that public libraries must be kept out of politics and politics out of public libraries has had a long-standing tradition. This tradition originated in Boston in the mid-nineteenth century and continues to be one of the guiding assumptions of public library policy and public library administration.

The reform in municipal government in the Progressive Era in the early years of this century perpetuated this myth. It was held that public librarianship ought to be a unique, autonomous, and nonpolitical function of government. This could be achieved through a separate governmental structure. The elimination of party politics in many municipal governments, including the switch from ward representation to at-large representation (through appointment or election) of library board members, the scheduling of elections for library boards at different times from other municipal elections, and the development of the position of library administrator are the consequences of the municipal reform movement. The model of efficient business enterprise provided the inspiration for municipal reformers. The purpose of the change was to develop library governments which would emphasize centralization, efficiency, expertise, professionalism, nonpartisanship, and nonpolitical control.

The preference for at-large appointment or election of public library board members was based on the "unitary myth." Considering the community as an organic whole, board members had to be given a citywide constituency, rather than be dependent on local neighborhood interests and the "corrupt" politics of such political arenas.[1]

The tenets of professional reforms in public librarianship have been:

1. A library board should be a corporate board rather than a political forum. Board members should be those who are best qualified by training, experience, and devotion to the public library to make policy. However, the library board should only be concerned with the broad outlines of library policy.

2. The administration of public libraries should be left to "neutral competence" of "disinterested" professional library administrators, and experts in library science, who claim command of the necessary expertise. Librarians insist that they are the best judges of how the resources allocated to the public library should be employed, and that they should control public libraries. Since library matters are essentially technical, lay library board members should defer to the library administrators who are qualified to make such decisions.

3. Library systems should be large enough to provide a large fiscal base and to allow the realization of economies of scale and marshal adequate resources to provide the broadest possible set of library services.

4. Public library policy should be conducted autonomously and in isolation from the political forces in its environment. Elections to library boards should be nonpartisan and separate from other elections. The public library should be impervious to pressure from external forces. Public library service must be separated from other governmental functions.

5. The public library is a local responsibility controlled by local officials.

Public librarians have usually followed the orthodox dogma of the separation of politics and administration. They have asserted that the public library should be controlled at the local level, but within the local community the public library should be protected from control or influence by other governmental officials. Keeping politics out of the public library has been based partly on its serviceability to public librarians. The myth of the separation of politics and public librarianship and the political patterns of public library governance is based upon a narrow definition of politics, confined to the two-party system. It has allowed the library professionals to keep considerable control of public librarianship in their hands, and at the same time to escape public accountability.

The politics of public librarianship is not unique. A governmental structure such as the public library can never be neutral. No matter how it is designed, the public library tends to benefit some groups more than others.[2] "To the degree that a political myth contrary to fact reflects the ideal rather than the real world of politics, and to the degree that the myth is believed by some, those who know the reality have a political advantage."[3] The at-large and nonpartisan appointed or elected library board has been less vulnerable to the political machine, but it has also served to ensure the persistent and pervasive political control of the public library by the middle class. But if the single most important key to political influence is political patronage, than public libraries are still open to such influence.[4] The patterns of library governance have been remarkably resistant to change. Pressure groups within local communities have seldom succeeded in having an impact on the governance of the local public library.

Public librarianship evolved into a paradox. The public library, which was heralded as an instrument of democracy, has in general rejected the political world in which democratic institutions operate and has insisted on independence from any other agency or instrument of local government.[5] But since political decisions affect public library programs, public librarianship is obviously political.

Public librarians are becoming aware of the increasingly political nature of public librarianship. The myth of the apol-

itical public librarianship no longer has any utility. Its serviceability is becoming limited. The effectiveness of this myth
rests on three critical elements: (1) those who propagate it must
not believe it themselves; (2) others must believe and respect
it; and (3) it must have functional utility.[6] None of these elements remain valid today. Public librarians have come to realize that they must become political.[7] A recent textbook on
local public library administration illustrates this point:

> The success of a library administrator depends largely upon an
> understanding of and an ability to operate within the context of the
> political process. Library administrators have, in many instances, held
> themselves aloof from politics, ignoring political reality and thus al-
> lowing the political aspects of library service to be handled elsewhere.
> ... It has become evident that this attitude has cost public libraries
> severely, in both status and financial capability. A failure to under-
> stand and utilize political processes has resulted in the lack of needed
> legislation and adequate tax support for public libraries.[8]

Although many public librarians have come to believe the
myth of the apoliticity of the public library, the reality always
was, and to a growing degree is, that public libraries are political institutions and part of the political system. Since the
public library is not a unique form of government or public
service, and since public librarianship is related to politics, the
politics of public librarianship promises to increase our knowledge of the public library and the links between public libraries
and politics. It may also provide public librarians with help in
tackling some of the problems faced by public librarianship
today.

NOTES

1. Robert H. Salisbury, "Schools and Politics in the Big City," *Harvard Educational Review* 37 (Summer 1967): 408–424.
2. William L. Boyd, "Rethinking Educational Policy and Management: Political Science and Educational Administration in the 1980s,"
American Journal of Education 92 (November 1983): 6.
3. Frank W. Lutz and Laurence Iannaccone, *Understanding Educational Organizations: A Field Study Approach* (Columbus, Ohio:
Charles E. Merrill, 1969), p. 13.

4. Bryan D. Jones, *Governing Buildings and Building Government: A New Perspective on the Old Party* (University: University of Alabama Press, 1985), p. 149; E. R. Shipp, "Politics, Lost Books and Budget Woes Vexing Chicago Libraries," *New York Times*, December 4, 1985.

5. Roscoe C. Martin, *Government and the Suburban School* (Syracuse, N.Y.: Syracuse University Press, 1962), p. 89.

6. B. Dean Bowles, "The Power Structure in State Education Politics," *Phi Delta Kappan* 49 (February 1968): 339.

7. Terry Schwadron, ed., *California and the American Tax Revolt: Proposition 13 Five Years Later* (Berkeley: University of California Press, 1984), p. 164.

8. Phyllis I. Dalton, "The Library and the Political Processes," in *Local Public Library Administration*, ed. Ellen Altman (Chicago: ALA, 1980), p. 29.

2

Public Librarianship and National Policy

Federal, state, and local governments are involved in the formulation and implementation of public library policies. One might view what is unique and what is typical about the politics of public librarianship by placing it in the broader context of public policy.

Public policy is an authoritative and goal-directed governmental course of action that states an intention to do something about a public problem. The Library Service and Construction Act adopted by Congress and signed by the President is an example of a public policy. It announces the intention of the federal government to do something about the lack or the inadequacy of public library service in the United States.[1]

The policy process, that is the various processes by which public policy is formed, can be divided into several stages: issue definition, policy agenda, policy formulation, policy adoption, policy implementation, and policy evaluation.[2]

POLICY MAKERS

Various participants within the three levels of government play important roles in the policy process. These participants are involved to a different degree in the various policy levels

Table 1

Participants in Public Librarianship Policy Making

	National	State	Local
General Legislative	Congress	State Legislature	Council
Public Librarianship Legislative	Congressional Subcommittee	State Library Board	Local Library Board
Executive	President	Governor	Mayor/ City Manager
Administrative	Department of Education	State Library Agency	Library Administrator
Professional Interests	ALA	State Library Association	Local Union

Source: Based on Stephen K. Bailey and Edith K. Mosher, ESEA: The Office of Education Administers a Law (Syracuse, N.Y.: Syracuse University Press, 1968), p. 232.

and in the several stages of the policy process within a political subsystem; a pattern of interactions between participants involved in making decisions in a particular area of public policy. Subsystems are important because they provide a channel through which nongovernmental groups can participate in the determination of policy. On the national level, the principal groups involved in the formulation and adoption stages of the public policy process are the education subcommittees of Congress and the primary library interest group, the American Library Association (ALA). In the implementation stage, they are the federal library agency and the state library agencies. On the state level, the principal group in the formulation stage is the state library association, and in the implementation stage, the state library agency. On the local level, the principal participant in all stages of the policy process is usually the library administrator. A matrix illustrating this process is shown in Table 1.

ISSUE DEFINITION

The public librarianship issue was originated by the leaders of the American Library Association (ALA). This group defined and stated the problem and the strategies to be used in bringing this problem to the attention of authoritative decision makers in the federal government.

During the 1920s and the 1930s, library leaders became aware of the fact that a large number of Americans, particularly those living in rural areas, did not have any access to public library service. Others did not have adequate public library service. The ALA conducted a study in 1926 that revealed that 82 percent of the rural population did not have library service.[3] Similar studies followed later. In 1952 there were still 33 million people with no public library service, and an additional 35 million people with inadequate public library service.[4]

The major difficulty that library leaders faced was to make public officials aware of the problem; to convince them that the problem had broad consequences; to make public librarianship an issue which, although of minor significance to the general public, would appeal to all. Library leaders also needed an issue that would be perceived by a large number of people as a public problem that government should handle.

POLICY AGENDA

Only a few of the many problems in American society are selected for governmental action; only a few of the demands are placed on the policy agenda and become problems on which policy makers choose to focus. In his study of the Senate, Jack Walker identified three features that enhance the probability that an issue would be chosen:

First, an item's attractiveness increases if it has an impact on large numbers of people.... Second, convincing evidence must exist that the proposed legislation is addressed to a serious and real problem.... Third, the case for inclusion on the agenda will be greatly strengthened if an easily understood solution exists for the problem being addressed.[5]

Interest groups are among the more important factors in agenda setting. They may convince or compel policymakers to put their problem on the agenda. The ALA succeeded in making public librarianship a problem that would receive governmental attention. It succeeded in placing the problem of public librarianship on the federal agenda by convincing congressional representatives to deal with this problem and to introduce bills in Congress for that purpose. This proved to be a lengthy process. Some fifteen years elapsed before the issue was placed on the government agenda; another ten years passed before it was adopted as the Library Services Act in 1956. The lengthy process was not the result of any real opposition to the way in which the issue of public librarianship was defined by the ALA, but a question whether public librarianship was a problem that should be placed on the national policy agenda.

PROPOSAL FORMULATION

Formulating a policy involves the development of plans to alleviate some need. Policy makers must develop acceptable proposals for an appropriate course of action to deal with a public problem. Policy proposals are often developed by public officials such as the president, but they are also developed by interest groups. The actual formulator of the proposals to deal with the problem of public librarianship was the ALA, which then found favorably inclined congressional representatives to introduce the proposals in Congress. There were seldom competing proposals from other interest groups, although there were competing proposals from the executive branch.

The policy of federal aid to public libraries can be categorized as a redistributive policy, because it is using public authority to transfer benefits from one group to another group.[6] In some states, public libraries were not considered a state responsibility. Many state and local governments were unable (or unwilling) to solve the problem of the lack and inadequacy of public library service as defined by the library profession. The solution for the problem was, in the opinion of the library leaders, the provision of federal aid. This seemed to them to be the best and most pertinent action to deal with the problem, since "interest groups attempt to maximize their effectiveness while minimizing costs by taking their causes to Washington. A single legislative victory in the Capitol may result in a uniform policy throughout the nation, with much less effort than would be required for 50 separate lobbying efforts in the states."[7] The ALA began to work in the 1920s toward this aim. There were two reasons for the proposal: equalization and stimulation of state aid to public libraries, and reduction of disparities in public library service. There was opposition to federal aid to public libraries within the association itself from both librarians and state library agencies but the proponents of federal aid within the ALA were able to persuade the opponents to drop their opposition and to unite behind the proposal. They have done so by coming out strongly for and emphasizing state control of federal funds. The proposals for federal aid to public libraries "were always coupled with a strong commitment to assure state and local plans for their implementation."[8]

Following World War II, the ALA decided that the time was propitious to formulate its proposal for federal aid to public libraries. The first step was the establishment of an office in Washington, D.C., and the hiring of a director for that office. In his history of the ALA, Dennis Thomison noted:

Although many librarians felt an almost instinctive repugnance over the word *lobby* because of past experience, the Washington office was clearly meant to perform in this capacity. Following the lead of other organizations, ALA was going to strengthen its influence by establishing an office close to Congress.[9]

The second step was the formulation of a lobbying strategy. The executive secretary of the ALA, realizing that it would be difficult if not impossible to obtain congressional approval of a proposal for a comprehensive system of federal aid to public libraries, suggested "a more opportunistic approach to the problem."[10] One component of this approach was to concentrate on a narrow aspect of the problem which most needed federal aid— library service to rural areas, an aspect that also had an emotional appeal. The other component was to be "politically realistic" and to discover other, stronger political groups that would be willing to cooperate on this proposal.[11] The result was a proposal requesting federal aid for rural libraries and the creation of a coalition with farm organizations and rural leaders. Educational groups had already joined their influence to the cause. It was clear to members of Congress that the proposal was formulated by an interest group. Senator Lister Hill, who introduced the Public Service Demonstration Bill in the 79th Congress in 1946, stated: "This bill, of course, is a bill of the American Library Association, but I happen to have introduced it."[12]

Several members of Congress who became library advocates were also willing to introduce proposals for federal aid to public libraries on the national agenda. When the first bill did not pass, others followed. In the 81st Congress three library bills were introduced; in the 82nd Congress, eight bills; in the 83rd Congress, fourteen bills. In the 84th Congress, twenty-eight bills focusing on public libraries were introduced.

POLICY ADOPTION

Policy adoption is generally thought of as building majority support for a policy proposal in Congress.[13] The policy to provide federal aid to public libraries had finally been able to build such support and was enacted by the 84th Congress in 1956, against the opposition of the Eisenhower administration. The ALA was never able to convince the executive branch that federal aid to public libraries was a national concern. The Library Services Act (LSA) of 1956, the Library Services and Construction Act (LSCA) of 1964, and the various amendments and reauthorizations generally passed with little or no opposition in Congress. The sharpest opposition occurred in 1964, when the LSCA passed the House of Representatives 254 to 107 and the Senate 89 to 7.

The LSA provided federal aid only to rural public libraries. As a result, library leadership, particularly urban librarians, considered it unsatisfactory and began a lobbying effort to expand the scope of the federal aid. The LSCA and its amendments expanded the law to provide federal aid to urban libraries, construction of public library facilities, library cooperation, and special groups of public library users (Table 2).

Table 2

The Library Services and Construction Act, 1956–84

Public Law 84-597   June 1956
                     Library Services Act (LSA) provided for
                     the extension and improvement of public
                     library services to rural populations (any
                     place of 10,000 population or less).

Public Law 86-679   August 1960
                     LSA extended for a period of five years.

Public Law 88-269   February 1964
                     Library Services and Construction Act
                     (LSCA) removed the population limitation
                     and extended the Act to all areas of the
                     country. Added Title II, for construction
                     of new public library buildings.

Public Law 89-511   July 1966
                     LSCA extended for five years. Added Title
                     III, interlibrary cooperation, for the
                     establishment and maintenance of
                     interstate, state, regional and local
                     networks of libraries, and Title IV, for
                     specialized state library service to
                     state institutions and to the physically
                     handicapped.

Public Law 90-154   November 1967
                     Permitted acquisitions of existing
                     buildings for public library use as
                     eligible expenditure under Title II.

Public Law 91-600   December 1970
                     LSCA extended for five years. Consolidated
                     Title I, IVA and IVB providing library
                     services to rural and urban disadvantaged,
                     provided for strengthening state library
                     agencies, strengthening metropolitan
                     libraries which serve as national and
                     regional resource centers. Streamlined
                     state plan procedures; removed matching
                     requirements for interlibrary cooperation.

Table 2 (*continued*)

Public Law 93-29	May 1973 Added new Title IV, "Older Readers Services." (Never funded).
Public Law 93-133	August 1974 Amended Title I, adding program priority for persons with limited English-speaking ability.
Public Law 95-123	October 1977 LSCA extended for five years. Adding emphasis on strengthening major urban resource libraries.
Public Law 98-480	October 1984 LSCA extended for five years. Current Title IV, "Older Readers Services" incorporated in Title I. Added new Title IV, providing library service to Indian tribes; Title V, for acquisition of foreign language materials; and Title VI, for library literacy programs.

Title I of the LSCA, the most important part of the public library legislation, provides funds

for the extension of public library services to areas without such services and the improvement of such services in areas in which such services are inadequate, for making library services more accessible to persons who, by reason of distance, residence, or physical handicap, or other disadvantage, are unable to receive the benefits of public library services regularly made available to the public, for adapting public library service to meet particular needs of persons within the States, for improving and strengthening library administrative agencies, and in strengthening major urban resource libraries.[14]

POLICY IMPLEMENTATION

Public laws are often ambiguous and vague. They are often endorsed without Congress carefully defining the problems that the law is supposed to address. The reasons are understandable. The demands and characteristics of the political process are frequently at odds with the methods that might yield more effective public laws. Members of Congress try to reconcile competing viewpoints in order to reach an agreement. The broader the language, the larger the group that can reach consensus. Goals are, therefore, vague in order to attain consensus. These goals are made operational through bargaining and compromise.

Federal administrators must translate the law into practice. The laws providing federal aid to public libraries gave the commissioner of education the formal authority and responsibility to implement them. But the objectives of the LSA and the LSCA were not precisely specified, nor were they ranked in order. As a result, the laws included two contradictory demands. One instructed the states to use the funds for specific programs outlined in the laws; the other gave the states complete discretion to use the funds in ways they saw fit. To the states, therefore, was reserved the power to decide the purposes to which they would use federal aid. Even when states applied their own priorities to the funds received from the federal categorical library grant, rather than pursue federal intentions, the federal library agency has had no legal or other recourse to prevent them. The ability of the federal government to influence the operation of the library categorical grant in the local public libraries was nil. Local public libraries had no power and no latitude as far as the federal aid was concerned. They had minimal input into the state decision-making process through a state advisory council on libraries, but these councils, required by the LSCA, were only advisory bodies, playing mostly peripheral roles.

The federal government and the majority of the states were not prepared for the implementation of the LSA. The Office of Education was isolated until the 1960s within the executive branch. It had a pervasive timidity, which was born of its fear that the the charge of federal control would be leveled against it. In 1956 the Office of Education was not ready to administer the LSA. The hierarchy of the Department of Health, Education and Welfare and the Office of Education had little concern about public librarianship. The Office of Education had to rely on the state library agencies in the writing of the regulations and guidelines for the implementation of the law. "State administrators were regarded by the Office of Education as colleagues who should have the maximum decision-making discretion permitted by categorical law."[15]

The main reason for placing the implementation of the LSCA in the hands of the states was to diffuse opposition in both Congress and the ALA to federal aid based on the fear of federal intervention in local public libraries. The plan adopted, however, "was not the result of any rational plan for federal intervention but rather an outcome of political bargaining and coalition formation."[16] The state library agencies were generally weak in the 1950s and, in some states, were nonexistent. The federal library agency produced regulations and guidelines for the states to reinterpret. As the funds flowed from Washington to the local public libraries, state priorities were substituted for federal priorities and much of the funds remained at the state level, rather than filtering to the local level.

The appropriation of funds by Congress has been another major aspect in the implementation stage of the federal library policy. With few exceptions, all administrations have requested in their annual budget requests less than was authorized by the act. Congress often increased the amount appropriated for the LSCA above the administration's budget request but seldom appropriated the full amount authorized. In fiscal years 1970 through 1975, for example, Congress authorized $622,775,000 for LSCA Title I. The administrations requested $117,969,000, and Congress appropriated $234,629,500. The appropriations were twice the administrations' requests but a third of the authorized amounts.

POLICY EVALUATION

In their study of policy implementation, Randall Ripley and Grace Franklin make the point: "Domestic programs virtually never achieve all that is expected of them."[17] Evaluation is an activity designed to judge the merits of a policy. The claims made for the impact of the LSCA have been inflated, and many of these claims were impressionistic. Reports on programs which were successful were published but the programs were seldom evaluated. The few evaluations commissioned by the federal library agency provide information on programs' out-

Table 3

Percent of Expenditure of LSCA Title I Funds, by Primary
Beneficiary Groups: Fiscal Year 1978

Primary Beneficiary Group	Percent
Urban Disadvantaged	2.5
Rural Disadvantaged	5.8
Urban and Rural Disadvantaged	1.6
Blind and Physically Handicapped Persons	6.2
Limited English Speaking Persons	1.3
Native Americans	0.5
Residents of State Supported Institutions	5.3
Special Target Groups*	5.2
Strengthening State Library Agencies	8.8
Strengthening Metropolitan Public Libraries	2.6
Strengthening Local Public Libraries	3.7
Public Librarians	2.6
The General Public	50.3
Cost of Administering the Act	3.9

*Including older persons, hearing impaired persons, children
and youth.

Source: Joseph Casey, Ronald Linehan, and Walter West, An
Evaluation of Title I of the Library Services and
Construction Act: Summary Report (Silver Spring, Md.:
Applied Management Sciences, 1981), p. 9.

puts but not their impacts. The effectiveness and impact of the
LSA and LSCA were not measured.

The problem of policy evaluation is the result of federal and
state agency and program officials' concerned about the possible political consequences of evaluation.[18] As a result, policy
evaluation of federal aid to public libraries tends to be policy
justification. Even the few evaluations that have been done,
including the one made by the General Accounting Office, have
been ignored by both the federal library agency and the state
library agencies. "Those who have an interest in the program

Table 4
Percent of Expenditure of LSCA Title I Funds, by Type of Agency:
Fiscal Year 1978

Agency	Percent
Local Public Libraries	35.2
State Library Agencies	31.9
Regional Public Libraries	23.0
State Supported Institutions	3.2
Other Public Agencies	4.5
Public & Multitype Consortia	2.2

Source: Joseph Casey, Ronald Linehan, and Walter West, An
Evaluation of Title I of the Library Services and
Construction Act: Summary Report (Silver Spring, Md.:
Applied Management Sciences, 1981), p. 6.

...are unlikely to lose their affection for it merely because an evaluation study concludes that its costs are greater than its benefits. Moreover, there is also the possibility that the evaluation may be wrong."[19]

The finding of the most recent evaluation of LSCA Title I has been "that both historically and in recent years, a significant proportion of available LSCA Title I funds have been expended on services that do not directly benefit the various priority groups identified in the Act"[20] (Table 3).

Direct expenditures of LSCA Title I funds for priority groups (targeted populations) identified in the act accounted for less than 20 percent in fiscal year 1978. It was estimated that two thirds of all public libraries have received no direct LSCA Title I grants, but almost all received some indirect benefit. Only 35 percent of the funds were used at the local level. (Table 4). This evaluation concluded that "there is a clear difference between expressed Federal level expectations and the reality of Program operations."[21]

CONCLUSION

The issues concerning a national policy of public librarianship have not been resolved. The direction and scope of the federal role are still being debated. Various arguments regarding such a policy have been set forth, and most of them deal with the question of federal aid. Proponents of this policy, such as the library interest groups, call for an increase in the scope of the programs, in the amount of money available, and in the role of the states in implementing the programs. Opponents, particularly the executive branch, call for the termination of the programs altogether.[22]

NOTES

1. Two recent surveys of federal library legislation are Edward G. Holley and Robert F. Schremser, *The Library Services and Construction Act: An Historical Overview from the Viewpoint of Major Participants* (Greenwich, Conn.: JAI Press, 1983); and Redmond Kathleen Molz, *National Planning for Library Service, 1935–1975* (Chicago: ALA, 1984).

2. James E. Anderson, David W. Brady, and Charles Bullock, III, *Public Policy and Politics in America* (North Scituate, Mass.: Duxbury Press, 1978), pp. 6–12.

3. Molz, *National Planning for Library Service*, p. 67.

4. Holley and Schremser, *The Library Services and Construction Act*, p. 17.

5. Jack L. Walker, "Setting the Agenda in the United States Senate," in *Congress and Public Policy*, ed. David C. Kozak and John D. Macartney (Homewood, Ill.: Dorsey Press, 1982), p. 445.

6. Theodore Lowi, "American Business, Public Policy, Case Studies, and Political Theory," *World Politics* 16 (July 1964): 677-715.

7. Deil S. Wright, *Federal Grants-in-Aid: Perspectives and Alternatives* (Washington, D.C.: American Enterprise Institute for Public Policy Research, 1968), p. 32.

8. Holley and Schremser, *The Library Services and Construction Act*, p. 6.

9. Dennis Thomison, *A History of the American Library Association 1876–1972* (Chicago: ALA, 1978), p. 163.

10. Carl H. Milam, "Federal Aid to Libraries," in *Library Extension: Problems and Solutions*, ed. Carleton B. Joeckel (Chicago: University

of Chicago Press, 1946), pp. 225–227.

11. Ibid.

12. U.S. Senate, Committee on Education and Labor, *Public Library Service Demonstration Bill.* Hearings before a Subcommittee on S. 1920. 79th Cong., 2nd sess., 1946. Quoted in Molz, *National Planning for Library Service*, p. 101.

13. Anderson et al., *Public Policy and Politics in America*, p. 10.

14. P.L. 91–600, sec. 110.

15. Frederick W. Wirt and Michael W. Kirst, *Schools in Conflict: The Politics of Education* (Berkeley, Calif.: McCutchan, 1982), p. 281.

16. Ibid.

17. Randall B. Ripley and Grace A. Franklin, *Bureaucracy and Policy Implementation* (Homewood, Ill.: Dorsey Press, 1982), p. 2.

18. James E. Anderson, *Public Policy-Making*, 3d ed. (New York: Holt, Rinehart & Winston, 1984), pp. 142–143.

19. Ibid., p. 143.

20. Joseph Casey, Ronald Linehan, and Walter West, *An Evaluation of Title I of the Library Services and Construction Act: Summary Report* (Silver Spring, Md.: Applied Management Sciences, 1981), p. 7.

21. Ibid., p. 26.

22. "Library Services and Construction Act: 97th Congress Reauthorization," Issue Brief 1B81064 (Washington, D.C.: The Library of Congress, Congressional Research Service), in U.S. House of Representatives, Committee on Education and Labor, Subcommittee on Postsecondary Education, *Oversight Hearings on Library Services and Construction Act*, October 19, 1981. 97th Cong., 1st sess., p. 235.

3

The Public Library in the Local Political Process

There were 8,639 public libraries in the United States in 1982. In that fiscal year, these public libraries spent over $2.3 billion, 79.2 percent of which came from local sources. State and local government expenditures for public libraries ranged from a low of $3.4 million in Vermont to a high of $262.8 million in California. Per capita expenditures ranged from a low of $3.42 in Arkansas to a high of $34.46 in Alaska (U.S. average was $8.61), and public library expenditures as a share of total state and local expenditures ranged from 0.24 percent in Georgia to 0.74 percent in Connecticut (U.S. average was 0.46 percent). Thirty-three states spent less than one-half of 1 percent of their total state and local government expenditures on public libraries.[1]

The majority of public libraries are small. Of the 8,639 public libraries, 5,495 (63.6 percent of total) serve fewer than 10,000 people, and 6,990 (80.9 percent) serve fewer than 25,000. Only sixty-three public libraries serve a population greater than 500,000. While they are decentralized in formal structure of control, public libraries show remarkable similarities. Of the 37,900 professional staff employed in 1982 in public libraries, only 21,600 (57 percent) had graduate library degrees.[2]

States, counties, municipalities, townships, and special districts are all purveyors of public library service. Public libraries, however, have long succeeded in keeping from the American public the fact that they are independent of the rest of local government. Over 90 percent of public libraries are a separate department within the local governmental structure.[3] The location of the public library in the local authority does not have any impact on the provision of library service. Public libraries under elected local officials, such as mayors, do not fare any better or any worse than public libraries under appointed officials such as city managers. Public libraries that are under an autonomous library board do not generally fare any better or any worse than public libraries that are departments of municipal or county governments.[4]

Because only a small percentage of local government finances are devoted to the public library (approximately 0.6 percent of total local governmental expenditures in fiscal year 1982), public library service has a low priority with city and county officials. "The traditional autonomy of the librarian, assured of financial support sufficient to maintain a kind of genteel poverty, has preserved the 'institution' from 'interference' from administrators in the past."[5] In California, for example, Proposition 13 forced greater proportional cuts in public library budgets than in any other major governmental service because public libraries were vulnerable, in large part because of the lack of political clout and organized constituencies in most libraries.[6]

LOCAL CONTROL

Local politics are crucial to public libraries because they can affect their quality, if not their very existence. Local governments decide whether or not to support a public library and the level of support that it will receive from local sources when they decide on the local government's priorities and the revenue to be raised for public services.

Local control has been a central feature and a hallowed principle of American political institutions. The most powerful advantage claimed for local control is that it endows citizens with independence and freedom in making decisions about their public services, including the public library. The basic idea is that democracy thrives when citizens are in close control of their own institutions. In theory, the public library is to be public in control. Yet in practice, public control is hard to define and even harder to accomplish.

The term "local control" is one expression of the fundamental value of individualism, which is characterized by a belief that the individual can best be protected if one can see what government is doing to one's interests. Legislative oversight is easiest at the local level, where policy makers are constantly before one's eyes and most easily reachable by election or referendum.

The deference to the norm that local communities should be the dominant partner in the American governmental system maintains a firm foothold in all the states. It means that the local public library should have the major voice in determining the goals and policies of public librarianship. Another result has been the decentralization of the public library. Since the 1960s, however, the states have been playing an increasing role in shaping public library policy. Local control is slowly eroding away and becoming meaningless.

COMMUNITY POWER

Different communities have different power structures, and power structure varies from community to community. Two types of community power structures have been suggested. One type is the elitist power structure, which sees power held by a small group of upper-class business leaders and other prominent citizens, who rarely hold any formal public office and who operate informally. The political machinery in the community, the elected officials, are subservient to the elite. The other type is the pluralist power structure, in which power is widely spread and shared among various groups and individuals in the community. Different individuals and groups are active in different issue areas and influence one another, and no one group dominates. Elected and appointed office holders predominate in decision making.[7]

The factors explaining the variations in community power

structure have been summarized by Philip Trounstine and
Terry Christensen:

1. City size and diversity. Larger and more diversified cities are more
   likely to have a pluralistic power structure. Small cities are less
   diversified and more likely to have an elitist power structure.
2. Economic diversity. As cities become more industrialized and un-
   ionized, their power structure becomes more pluralistic.
3. Structure of government. Cities with a mayor-council form of government, and partisan and district elections, are more pluralistic.
   Cities with a council-manager form of government and with at-
   large, nonpartisan elections have the elitist power structure.
4. Political culture comprising "the shared values, traditions, myths,
   and accepted behaviors of a community. . . . The values of the community affect who are acceptable as leaders and who the leaders
   listen to and care about, as well as whether the public is active or
   passive in community decision-making."[8]

   Those who hold power in a community are the ones who have
the ability to place issues on the political agenda, but more
importantly, they are also the ones who can prevent issues that
are contrary to their interests from becoming a part of that
agenda. The "nondecisions" are the questions that are never
asked, the issues that are never raised, and the policies that
are never seriously challenged.[9]
   The relevancy of a community's power structure to public
librarianship is slight. There is probably no informal "power
elite" (economic or otherwise) in public library politics. There
is little impact of the community power structure upon the
control of public library policy making. The ability to exert
influence and concert action on matters relating to public library service rests with persons who are involved in library
affairs because they hold (now or in the past) official positions
in the public library or in local government. Public library
policy is determined by professionals (and to a lesser extent,
by lay board members), generally subject only to scattered and
sporadic public pressures.

LOCAL GOVERNMENTS

Local governments have no legal status apart from state government. They are political subdivisions of the state, created by the state as "a convenient agency for the exercise of such of the governmental powers of the State as may be entrusted to it.... The state may withhold, grant, or withdraw powers and privileges as it sees fit."[10] The scope of legal authority enjoyed by local government units, however, varies among the states. State law gives permission to local governmental units to provide public library service, and this service is provided by all types of local governments. Public library service is provided by both general-purpose governments, such as counties, municipalities, and townships, which provide a range of public services, and by special-purpose governments, such as special districts, which are limited solely to the provision of public library service (Table 5).

Municipalities are still the most important type of local government in the provision of public library services. The importance of municipalities, however, has been declining since the 1960s, and the importance of both counties and special districts as providers of public library service has been increasing (Tables 6–8). Citizens believe that the way in which local government is structured determines to a large extent who will have how much access to local government officials and indeed who these officials are likely to be and to whom they will be most responsive.

MUNICIPALITIES

Municipalities are local government units officially designated as cities, towns, and villages, which are incorporated communities. Through incorporation a local community can gain control over various activities conducted within the community. It can also decide on the level of public services it wishes to provide and to direct these services according to community needs. Incorporation reflects the community's conclusion that alternative sources of needed services are less desirable or feasible.

Table 5

County, Municipal, Township, and District Governments Owning and Operating Public Libraries, by State, 1982

State	County	Municipality	Township	District
Alabama	17	88		
Alaska	4	8		
Arizona	8	43		
Arkansas	56	26		
California	53	106		27
Colorado	29	32		
Connecticut		16	81	
Delaware	3	2		
Florida	44	83		2
Georgia	65	51		
Hawaii				
Idaho	3	28		42
Illinois	4	218	42	107
Indiana	13	11	16	230
Iowa	16	115		6
Kansas	18	62	1	19
Kentucky	39	14		83
Louisiana	41	11		
Maine		16	54	
Maryland	20	4		
Massachusetts		35	204	
Michigan	29	132	111	
Minnesota	24	86		
Mississippi	38	56		
Missouri	27	54		51
Montana	32	17		
Nebraska	9	45	1	
Nevada	15	2		4
New Hampshire		12	61	
New Jersey	13	174	90	
New Mexico	7	31		
New York	9	83	89	
North Carolina	75	47		
North Dakota	8	12		
Ohio	15	18	6	48
Oklahoma	11	74		
Oregon	21	57		
Pennsylvania	12	92	39	1
Rhode Island		7	20	
South Carolina	35	8		
South Dakota	17	20		
Tennessee	61	38		
Texas	104	204		
Utah	14	24		
Vermont		7	24	
Virginia	50	38		
Washington	11	61		18
West Virginia	18	22		
Wisconsin	26	138	7	
Wyoming	19			

Note: All county governments and all library districts are included; municipal and township governments having population of more than 2,500. County governments include governments designated as boroughs in Alaska and as parishes in Louisiana.

Source: U.S. Bureau of the Census, 1982 Census of Governments: Vol. 1, General Governments (Washington, D.C.: GPO, 1983), Tables 8-9.

Table 6

Percent Distribution of Local Government Direct General
Expenditure for Libraries, by Type of Local Government, 1966–67,
1971–72, 1976–77

	1966–67	1971–72	1976–77
Counties	21	24	28
Municipalities	64	62	55
Townships	6	6	6
Districts	8	8	11

Source: Advisory Commission on Intergovernmental Relations,
State and Local Roles in the Federal System
(Washington, D.C.: GPO, 1982), Table 3.

Table 7

Percent Distribution of Local Government Direct General
Expenditure for Libraries in Metropolitan Areas, by Type of Local
Government, 1966–67, 1971–72, 1976–77

	1966–67	1971–72	1976–77
Counties	18	22	25
Municipalities	68	65	59
Townships	6	6	6
Districts	8	7	10

Source: Advisory Commission on Intergovernmental Relations,
State and Local Roles in the Federal System
(Washington, D.C.: GPO, 1982), Table 4.

Table 8

Percent Distribution of Local Government Direct General
Expenditure for Libraries in Nonmetropolitan Areas, by Type of
Local Government, 1966–67, 1971–72, 1976–77

	1966–67	1971–72	1976–77
Counties	23	37	47
Municipalities	50	42	36
Townships	8	6	4
Districts	11	14	15

Source: Advisory Commission on Intergovernmental Relations,
State and Local Roles in the Federal System
(Washington, D.C.: GPO, 1982), Table 5.

The most important development in municipal government since World War II has been the development of suburbs, and, as a result, the development of the suburban public library. The majority of suburbs and suburban public libraries are small because suburbanites wanted independent little suburban governments in order to get the municipal services they wanted, were able to pay for, could influence more easily, and could control locally. Of the 18,862 municipalities in existence in 1977, 9,614 had less than 1,000 people, and 15,282 less than 5,000.

"The central elements of the reform model of local government—a small city council elected at large on a nonpartisan ballot—continues to define politics in American cities." Over 70 percent of municipalities have nonpartisan elections, and two-thirds have at-large elections, although that number is decreasing. Some 78 percent of mayors are elected directly by voters.[11]

Municipalities are governed by a mayor, or a city manager, and a council in various combinations. Several forms of municipal government can be found: mayor-council, council-manager, or commission. In the mayor-council form of municipal government, the elected council serves as the legislative body. The mayor, elected separately, serves as the chief executive officer. The relative powers of the council and the mayor vary; mayors may be weak or strong vis-à-vis the council. More than 50 percent of municipalities, mostly in large and small municipalities, have the mayor-council form of local government. In the council-manager form of municipal government, which is most common in medium-sized municipalities, the council and the mayor make policy. The city manager is an appointed official who implements the policies and is responsible for the administration of the municipality and for the various departments of municipal government. The commission form of government exists in less than 3 percent of municipalities. It is composed of a board of elected commissioners, which is responsible for making policy and for the administration of the municipality. Each commissioner is responsible for one or more departments.

The structure of municipal government affects the pattern

of influence and often shows who has the dominant power in the municipality. The structure of city government is, however, less important than the elected or appointed officeholders of the municipality (the majority of whom are political amateurs) and the powers they exercise. Strong mayors, as well as many city managers, have powers that make them the chief administrative officers of their municipality. Mayors and city managers may have supervisory powers over the activities of the municipality's departments and are in charge of the preparation and administration of the budget. With the power of control over the budget the mayor or city manager can control and influence policies even within agencies that are otherwise independent and are controlled by a board, such as the public library. For their budgets, most public libraries are still dependent on the mayor and on the municipality's council, and most public library budgets are still a part of the overall municipality's budget. Even if the mayor has no powers of appointment and removal of the library administrator, he or she may have the power to appoint or remove public library board members. The fact that some appointments need the approval of the council is often of little significance as far as the public library board is concerned. Mayors, however, generally initiate few policy proposals. The majority of proposals brought before the council come from the municipality's bureaucracy and from various individuals or interest groups.

City managers who are appointed by the municipality's council and who are responsible to the council for the conduct of the administration of the municipality have significant power. City managers do not engage in direct political activities, but they are the policy innovators and policy leaders of their municipalities.

Although the manager plays a public role of "the expert" who is available only to answer questions and to administer, in practice, managers or their subordinates are the principal sources of policy innovation in cities today. Ideas, if managers or their staffs do not think of them in the first place, are likely to come, in most cities, from interest groups, rather than council members.[12]

COUNTIES

Counties were not established for the provision of public service but evolved as subdivisions of the state, created for the convenience of the state to carry out almost exclusively the general policy of the state. But in the Southern states, counties have been and continue to be where the local policy action exists.[13] Counties, however, have substantially expanded their activities since the 1950s. They have taken new responsibilities, beginning to operate more as local governments. Responding to the needs of their local populations, they have moved to provide additional public services, including public library service.

Over a third of the counties provide some kind of library service. In 1982, 1,133 counties (out of 3,041) provided library service (Table 9). Counties may provide library service to the entire county, or they may provide library service only to part of the county, for example, to areas not served by municipality or to unincorporated areas. Almost three-quarters of all metropolitan counties provide library service. In nonmetropolitan areas, municipalities surrender the leading share of library service to counties (Table 8). The role of the county in the provision of library service expanded dramatically following the modernization of county government since the 1950s.[14] In a survey of 1,026 counties conducted in 1971, the Advisory Commission on Intergovernmental Relations found that 56 percent of rural counties and 57 percent of urban counties provided public library service, and that this service ranked thirteenth out of fifty-eight functions.[15]

TOWNSHIPS

Townships were created as geographic subdivisions of counties and are found in only twenty states. Townships serve inhabitants in a defined area without regard to population concentration. Public libraries are among the most frequently reported township-owned and operated public services. Of 3,705 townships having a population of more than 2,500, 846 have a public library (Table 5).

Table 9

County Governments Owning and Operating Libraries, by
Population Size, 1982

Population	Number of Libraries
500,000 or more	35
250,000 to 499,999	47
100,000 to 249,999	100
50,000 to 99,999	156
25,000 to 49,999	226
10,000 to 24,999	314
Less than 10,000	255
Total	1,133

Source: U.S. Bureau of the Census, 1982 Census of Governments:
Vol. 1, Governmental Organization (Washington, D.C.:
GPO, 1983), Table 8.

LIBRARY DISTRICTS

Library districts have been the fastest-growing governmental unit in public library service. Between 1952 and 1982, the number of library districts has increased from 269 to 639. In 1982, there were library districts in thirteen states (Table 5). Like other types of special districts, library districts are independent, limited-purpose governmental units, which exist as separate entities and which have substantial fiscal and administrative independence from general purpose units of local government.[16] Library districts are generally also taxing districts, legally authorized to levy taxes.

Library districts are usually created after voters petition the county governing body, or the county court, which is followed by a public hearing and a referendum. In the majority of states, the library district's board of trustees is appointed, but in four states the board is elected. Library districts may also be established by special act of the state legislature.

The main distinction between library districts and other types of public libraries is that the library district is a totally independent taxing unit. The library board of trustees is empowered to levy tax, to borrow money, and to handle elections. The library district does not have to be tied to county, township, or municipal boundaries. It may have annexation powers and may annex surrounding territory.

Library districts are created for a number of reasons. The creation of a library district may permit the library to have a broader financial base to support library service than would be available to a general-purpose unit of government, such as a village. State governments have been responsible for stimulating the creation of library districts in some states as well.

The need for library service in a community where the general-purpose unit of government is not equipped or is unwilling to provide library service may lead to the establishment of a library district. Citizens with a strong preference for library service might not be able to receive it from their general-purpose unit of government because of the refusal or inability of that governmental unit to assume the responsibility for library service. Some local units of government are unwilling to provide library service for political reasons or because of conservative fiscal policies. Local government officials may be concerned that adding library service to the services provided by the local government will require additional revenues, which could be raised only through a library tax levy. This might incur the displeasure of the residents of their community. Furthermore, voters who might vote down a referendum for an additional tax levy might approve the creation of a library district to undertake that function and also approve the tax levy as part of the referendum. Indeed, the tax rate in library districts is often higher than in other types of public libraries. Because the boundaries of a library district are flexible and because it can extend beyond the boundaries of general-purpose government, library districts can overcome the limitation imposed by such boundaries and overlap existing political boundries.

There is a belief among citizens and librarians that by establishing library districts they are removing the library completely from possible influence and interference by partisan politics. Placing the library outside the purview of the general unit of local government, allowing the library freedom from external political pressure, and reducing the likelihood that political issues affecting the community will have an impact on the library help establish this independence. There is a desire among library professionals for complete independence from the local authority, making the public library accountable only to the voters. Creation of a library district is also a politically attractive solution that creates minimal disruption to existing governmental structures and political arrangements and can be created with only minimal alterations to the existing system of local government.

On the other hand, library districts are more vulnerable to budgetary constraints. In the aftermath of Proposition 13 in California, library districts fared much worse than libraries that were part of city and county governments.[17]

While conventional wisdom views special districts as inefficient and unresponsive and as governmental units that distort the political process by competing for scarce public resources, there is no evidence that library districts are any less effective or more responsive than are other types of public libraries.

SCHOOL DISTRICT LIBRARIES

School districts are local entities providing education. The majority are administratively and fiscally independent of any other governmental units. In a small number of communities, school districts also provide public library services. The school district libraries, however, are distinct from library districts because they are not independent governmental units. The school district is the taxing authority for the public library, which depends on the school district for its funds. Most school district libraries also operate under the board of education.[18] While the political unit in which the school district library is legally located is different from municipal or county public libraries, in reality that difference and its effect on the public library is minimal.

DISTRIBUTION OF PUBLIC LIBRARY SERVICE

The primary purpose of the public library is to provide library services to all citizens. The services are provided by the public library bureaucracy. The level of services provided to a community is largely determined by administrative decisions made by library administrators rather than by political criteria or voter choices. These administrative decisions produce bureaucratic rules, which are established to cope with service delivery. The service delivery rules are routinized procedures for accomplishing the goals of the public library. Public library bureaucratic decision rules are used to implement public library policies, so that a policy may be applied repetitively and routinely.[19] They are largely responsible for the pattern of public library service distribution. They determine what neighborhood receives what level of library service, and they tend to favor some groups over others.

When service delivery rules are technically and rationally related to the goals of a service delivery agency such as the public library, they are termed professional. Professional standards and norms dominate political considerations in public library service delivery. Library professionals are not susceptible to external influences in the development or implementation of public library service. Library decision making is largely devoid of explicit political content. The uniform application of service delivery rules provides the library bureaucracy with a defense against interference from the local authority, various groups, and the public. Efforts by elected officials, groups, or citizens to criticize the ways in which library services are distributed are resisted by reference to professional standards and norms.

The key measures of public service performance are efficiency, effectiveness, and equity. Efficiency is concerned with the costs of library service, and effectiveness with the objectives of library service. Library bureaucratic rules are established to resolve distributional issues in the name of efficiency and effectiveness. Decision rules simplify decision making, make for easier application of the rules, and limit discretion at the branch level and avoid conflict. Choices made by library administrators in their application of what appear to be sensible rules may have unintentional discriminatory effects:

> When the chief librarian sorts out his or her budget, he or she allocates resources among the branches of the library system according to the number of books circulating out of each branch. However, librarians also influence which books circulate because they determine what constitutes a "good" or balanced library collection. If needs of minority readers are not considered (for example, by the provision of foreign language or special history collections) then a branch library in a minority area may find that fewer books are circulating. That library, therefore, will be allocated fewer resources. Over time, the application of these professional norms can lead to the funneling of more and more library resources into middle class neighborhoods, leaving minority areas with inferior library services.[20]

Library bureaucrats rely on circulation rates as a guide to the distribution of services. That is, libraries with higher user levels receive a disproportionate share of available resources. The circulation rule is plausible in that it facilitates application, reduces uncertainty, relies on records typically maintained by library bureaucrats, does not require elaborate data collection and analysis procedures, and has the virtue of appearing to be fair. Another rule used by urban libraries to guide distributional policy is the provision of more resources to the central library for the purchase of library material than it would receive if total system circulation were used to distribute resources.

Several studies have investigated how public library service is distributed and what accounts for the differences in the treatment of some neighborhoods. *Access to Public Libraries* found that predominantly white neighborhoods had a greater probability of containing a branch library than predominantly nonwhite neighborhoods. The branches in nonwhite areas also had a less adequate book stock. Furthermore, predominantly high-income neighborhoods were more likely to have a branch than predominantly low-income neighborhoods. The pattern was unmistakable; low-income and nonwhite areas were generally served more poorly than the other areas.[21] Similar conclusions were reached by Lowell Martin in Chicago. The pattern of library facilities, personnel, and expenditures of the Chicago Public Library favored more advantaged neighborhoods. "The policy which prevailed...was to scale down provision of library service in a community if home circulation of books declined. Areas of low education and areas of rapid change were hit hardest of the policy....Thus the Library itself initiated a downhill spiral."[22] In Oakland, California, the study team of Frank Levy, Arnold Meltsner, and Aaron Wildavsky found that low-income areas received a smaller share of the benefits from the library branch system than their share of contribution to total tax revenues. They concluded:

While the educational and recreational needs of persons in middle- and upper-income areas are being met...those of lower-income persons are not. The combination of poor and often irrelevant collections, a small total branch budget, the vicious circulation-allocation cycle, and the consequent deterioration of poverty-area buildings means that the branch system provides little education or recreation for those city residents who need it most."[23]

The distribution pattern was the result of complex bureaucratic decision rules by library administrators; neutral-sounding bureaucratic routines led to unequal allocation of library resources. "What surfaces are the professional mores of librarians...as to their conception of how to deliver a service properly and how to treat various categories of consumers."[24]

The distribution of library resources and services in Houston strongly favored upper-income areas. Branches in low-income neighborhoods received fewer books and periodicals, a smaller percentage of the total budget allocation, fewer librarians, and less qualified personnel. The location of the branches, on the other hand, favored low-income neighborhoods.[25]

Five primary explanations have been suggested as to why public services are distributed differently to various neighborhoods. Public library service to a certain neighborhood can be a function of:

1. the ethnic composition of the neighborhood;
2. the socioeconomic status of the neighborhoods;

3. the proportion of the neighborhood's population occupying positions
   of power in local government;
4. the ecological aspects of the neighborhood, such as its age, density,
   geographical character, and residential-commercial mix; or
5. bureaucratic decision-rules.[26]

There is nothing particularly "equal" about the distribution
of library services because they are, in the end, the result of
bureaucratic rules. The inequitable bureaucratic rules come
about because the library board allows the library bureaucracy
considerable discretion in the conduct of its affairs; the library
bureaucracy is relatively immune from demands from higher
authority, since few, if any, of its decisions are likely to attract
the attention of elected officials or groups, and the library system experiences few demands from citizens.

Equity refers to the fairness, impartiality, or equality of service. Several different, seemingly equitable formulas can be or
are used to allocate or distribute public services. For example,
the per resident expenditure in each public library branch
should be proportionate to the taxes paid by the residents in
the neighborhood served by the branch. Conversely, library
service could be assigned throughout the area in such a way
to produce equal results in the different neighborhoods, and
each branch would receive sufficient expenditure so that per
resident circulation is equal in all branches. Another formula
would give each branch an equal per resident expenditure.
Each formula is manifestly equitable in certain important re-
spects and inequitable in other, competing principles.

Several conceptions of equity can be applied to test the distribution of public library service, including need and demand.
When the concept of demand is applied as the test for equity,
the distribution of library resources seems an equitable arrangement. However, when the concept of need is applied as
the test for equity, the opposite is true.

There is a widely held belief that professionally determined
local public library service is determined according to politically neutral decision rules and that professional standards
dominate political considerations in public library service delivery. Library bureaucracy is characterized by the fact that

many of its key decisions concerning public library service distribution are made by library personnel who are not elected and who are immune from many of the sanctions that might be used by elected political officials to encourage response to citizen demands.[27]

There is some evidence that politics can interfere with the bureaucratic service delivery process and that political forces can influence the bureaucratic procedures that normally account for patterns of service distribution. Some groups are better at manipulating bureaucratic procedures to gain their own ends. As a result, public bureaucracies do not neutrally implement public policies enacted by the policy-making branches of government. Even in cities with a strong political machine, however, public library service is not used often to reward supporters of the machine.

The lack of political pressure is also due to the public library's lack of a well-defined clientele group and the fact that existing library facilities limit the opportunity for discretionary behavior. Once a public library branch building is in place, it is hard to relocate it in response to changing configurations of electoral outcomes.

CONCLUSION

The public library is one of the public services provided by the various types of local government. As such, it is affected by the political institutions and processes that affect local government in general.

NOTES

1. "An NCLIS Library Statistical Sampler," *Library Journal* 110 (October 15, 1985): 35–36; David Sweet and Betsy Faupel, "Public Library Expenditures—FY 1981–82," *Public Libraries* 24 (Spring 1985): 15.

2. Robert A. Heintze, "The NCES Survey of Public Libraries, 1982," *The Bowker Annual of Library and Book Trade Information, 1985*, p. 414.

3. Barbara M. Robinson, "Municipal Library Services," *Municipal Year Book 1979*, pp. 63–64.

4. Margaret Lomer and Steve Rogers, *The Public Library and the Local Authority Organization and Management* (Birmingham, England: University of Birmingham, Institute of Local Government Studies, 1983).

5. Robert H. Salisbury, "Trends in Urban Politics and Government: The Effects on Library's Functions," in *The Metropolitan Library*, ed. Ralph W. Conant and Kathleen Molz (Cambridge, Mass.: MIT Press, 1972), p. 152.

6. Alvin Rabushka and Pauline Ryan, *The Tax Revolt* (Stanford, Calif.: Hoover Institution Press, 1982), pp. 123–124.

7. Philip J. Trounstine and Terry Christensen, *Movers and Shakers: The Study of Community Power* (New York: St. Martin's Press, 1982), pp. 24–40.

8. Ibid., pp. 40–47.

9. Peter Bachrach and Morton S. Baratz, *Power and Poverty: Theory and Practice* (New York: Oxford University Press, 1970), pp. 43–46.

10. *City of Trenton v. State of New Jersey*, 262 U.S. 182 (1923).

11. Heywood T. Sanders, "The Government of American Cities: Continuity and Change in Structure," *The Municipal Year Book 1982*, p. 186.

12. Charles R. Adrian and Charles Press, *Governing Urban America*, 5th ed. (New York: McGraw-Hill, 1977), p. 201.

13. Vincent L. Marando and Robert D. Thomas, *The Forgotten Governments: County Commissioners as Policy Makers* (Gainsville: University Presses of Florida, 1977), pp. 1–2.

14. Carolyn B. Lawrence and John M. DeGrove, "County Government Services," *The County Year Book 1976*, p. 98.

15. Advisory Commission on Intergovernmental Relations, *Profile of County Government* (Washington, D.C.: GPO, 1972), pp. 22–25.

16. David Shavit, "Library Districts in Illinois," *Illinois Libraries* 66 (October 1984): 430–435.

17. *Tax Revolt Digest*, January 1979, quoted in Rabushka and Ryan, *The Tax Revolt*, p. 126.

18. Alex Ladenson, *Library Law and Legislation in the United States* (Metuchen, N.J.: Scarecrow Press, 1982), pp. 45–50.

19. Bryan D. Jones, *Governing Buildings and Building Government: A New Perspective on the Old Party* (University: University of Alabama Press, 1985), p. 128.

20. Astrid E. Merget and William M. Wolff, Jr., "The Law and Municipal Services: Implementing Equity," *Public Management* 58 (August 1976): 5–6.

21. International Research Associates, Inc., *Access to Public Libraries* (Chicago: ALA, 1963).

22. Lowell Martin, *Library Response to Urban Change: A Study of the Chicago Public Library* (Chicago: ALA, 1969), p. 76.

23. Frank S. Levy, Arnold J. Meltsner, and Aaron Wildavsky, *Urban Outcomes: Schools, Streets and Libraries* (Berkeley: University of California Press, 1974), p. 200.

24. Astrid E. Merget, "Equity in the Distribution of Municipal Services," in *Revitilizing Cities*, ed. Herrington J. Bryce (Lexington, Mass.: Lexington Books, 1979), p. 176.

25. Kenneth R. Mladenka and Kim Quaile Hill, "The Distribution of Benefits in an Urban Environment: Parks and Libraries in Houston," *Urban Affairs Quarterly* 13 (September 1977): 73–94.

26. Robert L. Lineberry, *Equality and Urban Policy: The Distribution of Municipal Public Services* (Beverly Hills, Calif.: Sage, 1977), pp. 57–67.

27. Kenneth Mladenka, "The Urban Bureaucracy and the Chicago Political Machine: Who Gets What and the Limits to Political Control," *American Political Science Review* 74 (December 1980): 996.

4

The Politics of Public Librarianship at the Local Level

Since the middle of the nineteenth century, public library governance has been based on the principle that the public library is a public function, rooted in state statutes but administered by local officials. The public library is a state function but a local responsibility. Each state has complete authority for public library service within its boundaries. Each state has one or more general public library laws, and each state, except Hawaii, delegates the responsibility for public library service to local authorities.

Public libraries are generally one of the public services provided by local governments. Only a small percentage of public libraries are "independent," having authority to raise revenue and function without obligatory reference to other units of local government operating in much of the same territory or serving some or all of the same population. All other public libraries are "dependent" on general-purpose units of local government, such as counties, municipalities, or townships.

POLICY-MAKING PROCESS IN THE LOCAL PUBLIC LIBRARY

The stages of the policy-making process in the local public library are similar to those outlined in chapter 2. Proposals for action are formulated when needs are articulated. The demands for action may come from outside the public library; from local individuals or groups, or even from the state or the federal government. The policy proposals are, however, generally proposed by the library administrator and are based on professionally articulated demands for specific public library services and activities. The library administrator will place the demands on the library agenda and will suggest the alternative responses to the demands. The library board may consider the various policy alternatives proposed by the library administrator. The agenda setting, that is, the introduction of topics for discussion at the library board meetings "is the opening round in the struggle for influence, and by no means an inconsequential one."[1] The agenda setting in the public library is largely in the hands of the library administrator, insulated from involvement by the public. If the public enters the policy-making process, it does so generally only after the issues have been defined and the agenda has been set. The library administrator will usually establish an agenda that will minimize controversy and maximize problems that require routine administrative resolution.

The recommendations for policy and for action made by the library administrator to the library board are generally expected and honored. "Indeed, it appears only reasonable that those who set the agenda should also recommend appropriate policy actions."[2] Furthermore, the actions approved by the board will have to be implemented by the library administrator, and any political conflicts arising from the board decisions will have to be resolved by the library administrator. Therefore, the library board will usually reach decisions based on the administrator's policy proposals. While the public may attend and participate in the board meeting, it plays an insignificant role in it.

The actions approved by the library board are implemented by the library administrator and the professional staff of the public library. "It is at the implementation phase of governance that linkages between policy intent and policy achievement can be most easily modified by professional hostility."[3] This is also true in regard to the evaluation of library policies and programs. Evaluation of programs involves comparing the performance of these programs with their objectives. Such evaluations are seldom made in the public library because library boards do not have the staff or the expertise to conduct them. They must rely on the library staff who have implemented the policy to evaluate it as well. Reviews by external agencies, such as the state library agency, are weak or nonexistent.

THE LIBRARY BOARD

Over 90 percent of public libraries in the United States are governed by library boards. The vast majority of public library boards are appointed by elected local officials, such as the mayor or the city council, or the mayor with the approval of the council. Members of some library boards are elected by the local citizenry, often in special elections. In some cities, the board of education serves as the public library board or appoints the library board. Regardless of the way it is established, the library board is probably the least visible of community bodies. In most communities, the library board also has a low status.

The library board is both a creature of the state and a local institution. It is both a policy-making and an administrative body for the public library. The board acts in the interest of the local public library (whose public it is presumed to represent) while implementing the mandates of the state. The authority of the library board lies in its corporate body, not in its individual members. The role of the library board member is similar to that of the school board member and

is perhaps the most ill-defined in local government. The individual board member has no legal power, though the board itself is considered a corporation. The board's rights and responsibilities are rarely spelled out by the state except in the most general terms, and the board rarely undertakes to define them itself. The board's entire role and that of its individual members is simply an accretion of customs, attitudes, and legal precedents without much specificity. Many ... board members ... move in a sea of confusion about their powers.[4]

Selection of Board Members

Like the recruitment of councilmen to city council, the recruitment of members to the library board is based on a "strong norm of volunteerism." City councilmen "treat council service as a 'citizen duty' in much the same manner as they treat service on the Chamber of Commerce, the PTA, the Library Board, and other such community service organizations. . . . Although the volunteer in office, especially if relatively indifferent to staying there, may be a devoted public servant as he defines the role, he is unlikely to be constantly sensitive to voters' preferences."[5]

Appointment to the board is often based on personal acquaintance between the appointee and a member of the appointing body (such as the mayor or the city council). Appointment to the library board may also be a political reward. However, these appointments are not considered by the appointing body to be decisions of major importance.[6]

The library board is considered to be a representative body through which local control is exercised, but it is not. It is generally unresponsive and undemocratic. It is particularly less responsive to ethnic and low-income groups. The concept of "taxation without representation" seems to be applicable to most public libraries. Furthermore, library board members in most communities do not represent clearly visible constituencies. Although they are appointed or elected to represent the community in making local library policies, library boards represent only a small proportion of the community. Basically, they represent the well-educated middle class; they are "elite" board members, better off economically than the community average. Even in communities that have elected library boards, board members have no visible constituencies who support their candidacies and ensure their election. Nor is there any strong constituency that watches their behavior after the election. Library board members do not have to report to their community (except for the library's annual report) and therefore have considerable freedom in their behavior.

Library board elections are nonpartisan and are notorious for the paucity of issues and sometimes even for the dearth of candidates. The lack of issues (or candidates) in library board elections testifies even more to the absence of constituencies, although the lack of participation and competition in library board elections is not unique to this agency. There is no evidence that elected library boards are more representative of or more responsive to their communities than appointed boards.

From the mid-1930s to the mid-1970s, only small changes occurred in the composition of library boards. In 1960 Morton Kroll reported that library board members were not representative of the communities they served.[7] Kroll also found that library board members were of a "secondary echelon of community elite," close to power but not themselves powerful.[8] The Illinois library board member in 1983 was well-educated, aged fifty or more, with an annual income in excess of $30,000. The only major difference from previous boards has been the fact that female board members outnumbered male members. Sixty-eight percent of library board members in Texas and 65 percent in Illinois in 1983 were women.[9]

The major changes have been the decrease in the number of businessmen and professionals, and the increase in the number of homemakers, retirees, and administrators. Board members are also getting younger, although the majority are still over fifty years of age. Library board members are also serving shorter periods of time. Ann Prentice found that more than 50 percent of members served less than five years. But much of the change has occurred in small communities; public library boards in large urban communities are more similar to the traditional pattern. In the large public libraries in Illinois, male board members are still in the majority. They were also better educated and had higher annual incomes. A very small percentage of board members are from minority groups.[10]

Preentry experience to library board membership is limited to participation in various community activities, which give the library board members exposure in the community. The political potential of library board membership is almost nil. Library boards are of minor political importance to the community.[11] Prentice found that library board members had slight impact on the political structure of their community.[12] Since the service is voluntary, board members see it as a discharge of duty and as a source of status rather than as a stepping stone in a political career. From the point of view of political involvement, library board members are not active, nor are they in a strategic position to exert political pressure.

Cavalierly appointed and similarly regarded, they often have a hard time convincing friends in city or county government of the importance of their impoverished charge. Nor can it be said that, generally speaking, they burn with a desire or feel a sense of crisis sufficient to fight for the library's program.[13]

The result of the fact that library boards are not politically active has been summarized as follows:

Since ultimately the library is dependent upon elected officials for the amount of its tax support, the generally marginal level of trustee participation in this area is probably not in the best interest of library service . . . if the trustee were more active politically, he might be able to widen the base of library support and thus have a stronger position when competing with other agencies for funds.[14]

A few public libraries have a self-perpetuating board, in which board members appoint their own successors. Such boards generally do not have autonomy in budgetary matters. The self-perpetuating board in general runs the risk of "withdrawing from the political process to such an extent as to endanger its ability to obtain sufficient public funds for the support of the library."[15]

The Culture of Local Library Boards

Library boards share a political culture of their own, based on traditions, norms, and values that were developed in the second part of the nineteenth century.

Most library board members come to their positions with little experience to guide them in their political roles. The traditions, norms, and institutions of library governance further insulate them from the political environment. They seek office for widely different reasons. A survey of library board members in Illinois disclosed that 42 percent of library board members served because of interest in books and libraries, 32 percent from civic duty, and 15 percent because they perceived the library to be of importance to the community. Seven percent were pressured into the position of library board member because no one else was willing to do it.[16] The social, economic, and political background of library board members and the conditions of entry partially explain how members will behave once they are on the library board. Gellert found that some board members exerted more influence than others because they possessed more knowledge, had the right political and social connections, or had more economic resources than the other board members.[17] Library board members behave in ways similar to school board members:

Amazingly, the vast majority of these persons end up behaving as board members in very similar ways. They tend to meet in private to work out the "right" solution to any and all problems; they try to come to decisions that are equally good for *all* the people; they usually enact their policies in unanimous fashion in public; and they shun any behavior that looks like special interest representation.[18]

These points are made clear in a handbook to library board members. For example, the handbook states that "trustees should . . . be governed by *esprit de corps* outside the board room," and that "disagreements among board members should not emerge from the board room, to the public detriment of the library."[19] It is important to the library board to present a facade of unanimity to the public.

Library board members generally do not have close affiliations with political parties, and the attitude of library board members is generally that public libraries should be sheltered from the "contaminating" influence of politics. Board members will not lobby willingly, and since they are generally appointed by a public official because of personal acquaintance, they will generally refrain from any activity that will embarrass that official. "No matter what the legal status of the library board it would be unlikely that they would be willing to operate as a pressure group."[20]

Library Board and the Community

Democratic appearances notwithstanding, direct influence of the public on public library governance is practically non-existent, but not because citizens do not have available access. Channels of communication are available to the citizens. Board elections, open board meetings, board members, and the library administrator are reachable. But voter turnout at library board elections is very low, and few citizens come to board meetings.

While direct participation in the public library is more possible in libraries that elect their board members (since elected members may be more accountable to the public than appointed ones), there is no discernible difference between elected and appointed boards.

Library boards try to arrive at a consensus in private. Statements in handbooks for library board members exhort them that "loyalty to library welfare will not encourage either schisms on the board or feuds within the community," that "a united front should be presented to the public," and that "the library board has the responsibility of leading an active campaign to educate the voters of the community about library needs."[21]

While library board members consider themselves as servants of the public trust, who govern the public library as a public trust, they do not consider themselves as representatives of the public or responsible to it, but as trustees. Board members consider the public library, not the public, of paramount concern to them. Most library board members "do not view themselves as representatives communicating constituent preferences to administrators. They view their tasks as legitimizing decisions made by administrators, publicizing administrative decisions, and generating public support for those policies."[22]

There are few demands from the community. Indeed, there are seldom any demands for community control of the public library.

Library Board and Library Administrator

Like the relationship between school board and school superintendent, the relationship between the library board and the library administrator is inherently one that cannot be defined precisely and that injects an element of uncertainty into the organization and its operations. The fact that any sharp dichotomy between policy formulation and administration is unreal makes it all the more difficult to implement the notion that the board should function in a purely policy-making or quasi-legislative capacity and keep itself aloof from the administrative processes that give full meaning to programs, policies, and standards.[23]

According to popular folklore, the public library board sets policy, and the library administrator and other professional staff of the library implement that policy. The formal authority of administering the public library belongs to the board, which is legally the policy-making body for the public library. It is the body which has the power to hire and fire the library administrator, but the library administrator has the technical authority. Like public school decision making, public library decision making is dominated by library administrators who control the information and who can manipulate institutional arrangements to their political advantage.[24] The library board does not govern but mainly legitimizes the policy recommendations of the library administrator. "The board becomes an agent of legitimation that provides a facade of public control, while power is really exercised by administrators."[25] The library administrators, while insisting they are held in check by the board, are charged with educating the board in library matters, and establish a monopoly on technical knowledge and information.

The technical expert... is likely to flourish in those community settings where *expertise* and division of labor are assigned intrinsic value. ... [The library administrator] brings to his job information, skills, and his entire occupational attention. Where his "employers" on the board and in the community trust and value *expertise*, he is likely to have much discretion and initiative, right up to the highest policy level.[26]

The rights and responsibilities of the library board are not spelled out in public library legislation except in general terms. The law does not define the role of the individual library board member. Indeed, while the board has corporate power, individual board members have no legal power whatsoever. Public support is given to the public library and not to the library board. Library administrators understand that board members do not really represent the public. Library board members defer to the expertise of the professional library administrator. Indeed, library trustee associations tell library board members to accede to the administrative judgment of the administrator.

Library boards typically enact policies suggested by the professional staff. The agenda of the board meetings is generally prepared by the library administration, sometimes in consultation with the board chairman. Both library board members and library administrators believe that board members are incapable of effective governance. Directors work hard to insure minimal input from boards. Indeed, many library administrators have developed a talent of circumventing real board participation in policy activity. For example, the library administrator will fill the board's agenda with routine matters, so that it does not have the time, even if it had the inclination, to deal with more important issues unless they are placed on the agenda by the library administrator.

Library administrators believe that because library boards, being laypersons, lack the necessary expertise, they cannot or will not govern. The majority of library administrators do not really want board members to have a significant role in policy formation. Library administrators view themselves as the true policy makers and view the library board as a necessary evil. Conflicts between library board and library administrators usually involve the definition of the role of each vis-à-vis the other. Like city managers, library administrators define "policy" and "administration" in such a way that "administration" turns out to bulk very large and "policy" is very small.[27] Library board members do not necessarily disagree with the library administrator's view.

Library board members consider their paramount task the employment of a library administrator. (Making library policy comes second.) Furthermore, "board members must at all times demonstrate their loyalty to the librarian" and "the librarian should be able to rely upon the backing of the board in carrying out the policies of the library."[28] There is, however, a point at which the board and the administrator must part company. Robert Alvarez found that 13 percent of library administrators were fired or asked to resign.[29] Such terminations usually result from unreconcilable disagreements between the library board and the library administrator.

A study of library boards in Illinois showed that "the actions taken at...board meetings differ markedly from what we would expect by knowing which duties the trustees say are most important."[30] The study found great discrepancy between what the board members said was important and what was emphasized most during board meetings. The activity that occurred most frequently in board meetings was reviewing current library activity. This activity was not even mentioned by board members as an important task but is often used by library administrators to manipulate the board's time. As a result, the responsibilities ranked highest by library board members, such as improving library service and policy making, are seldom dealt with in board meetings. "Board members perform first those tasks which are simple and readily definable— regardless of their perceptions of the tasks' importance."[31] As a result, the library board and its monthly meetings are not the primary locus of decisions leading to the formulation of public library policy."[32]

Regardless of library administrators' views of library boards, it should not be assumed that library administrators favor the elimination of the library board. The opposite may be true. The library administrator needs the board as an agency of legitimation and as a shield. The library board shields the library administrator through the myth of the apoliticity and the local control of the public library. The library board can be a mechanism drawing away excessive criticism. Without it, the library administrator is more open to public attack. One of the major reasons that library administrators prepare book selection policies for the approval of their board is to shield them from such public attacks.

Again, Virginia Young's handbook for library board members makes its clear that "the trustee's devotion to the welfare of the library should ensure the board standing shoulder to shoulder as a solid entity behind its policies and behind the librarian in carrying out those policies,"[33] that "devotion to the library and its welfare should weld the board into solid backing for the librarian,"[34] or that "it is the board's moral obligation to stand behind the librarian in carrying out policies. Boards are most frequently called upon to support policies in the field of public relations and of book selection."[35] Library administrators usually socialize new board members to the workings of the board, and there is usually pressure on library board members to conform. The emphasis is not on the board being a spokesperson for the community to the public library, but rather on the board becoming a spokesperson for the library administrator to the community and having the board and the library administrator establish a united front against outside criticism.

The reasons for the ascendancy of the library administrator over the library board are the separation of library governance from municipal governance and the acceptance of the normative proposition that public library issues are technical matters rather than political issues, and that library administrators are better qualified to make technical judgments. "An administrator, by claiming that the ground of his decisions are 'purely professional,' may be able to resist the claims of those interest groups which, for one reason or another, it is convenient for him to resist, as well as the directions of his political superiors."[36]

LIBRARY ADMINISTRATORS

Like city managers and school superintendents, public library administrators "are professionally trained experts held accountable to lay legislatures."[37] Library administrators have a stake in the idea that the delivery of public library service is essentially technical and that decisions should be made by those with technical expertise.

Although library administrators are legally subordinate employees of the lay library boards, which are representatives of the public and should be accountable to it, those boards are no match to the library administrators. Professional librarians hold the belief that they are under the nominal control of those who are incompetent to judge professionals' performance. Most decisions in the public library are made by library administrators with the concurrence of the library board. In terms of de facto power, lay library boards are no match for professional library administrators who have more expertise, longer tenure, and full-time involvement in their work.

Library administrators have detailed knowledge of the library, its operation, and its services. The library boards do not have and rarely acquire such detailed information. Interest groups do not have the necessary knowledge and are at a disadvantage in any conflict with the library administrator. The library board has no staff of its own to assist it. It must rely on the library staff and on the information supplied by that staff, which is controlled by the library administrator. When interest groups try to rely on the board for the information they need, they, too, have to rely on the library administrator and staff. Providing the library board with a separate staff to assist it in its decision making (similar to the staff of some legislative bodies) would be resisted by the library administrator, because a separate staff for the library board would create a competing center of expertise.[38]

The belief accepted by the library profession is that library administrators should be politically neutral but technically competent, that library administrators are experts and that part of their authority rests in being "above politics." Library administrators demand, therefore, that they should be shielded by the board from the winds of public opinion. As a result, pluralist democracy comes into conflict with professional beliefs about administrative efficiency, and there is an inherent tension between professionalism and responsiveness.

Contrary to the professional maxim that library administrators not engage in politics, library administrators, like school superintendents and city managers, are political and hold political power.[39] They are politicians because they are involved with policy making. Being a library administrator involves the manipulation and exercise of organizational power, essentially a political activity. Library administrators must make decisions on controversial matters, and all such decisions involve subjective judgments about values. "Being a career man under civil service relieves the administrator of the necessity of participating in party politics, but it does not relieve him of the necessity of making decisions which are politically significant."[40]

The fact that library administrators are generally hired by a semiautonomous board makes library administrators weak vis-à-vis the local political arena. Library administrators have little or no political support to fight the mayor or city council, particularly on budgetary matters.[41] Furthermore, many library administrators find dealing with local government and with the political structure a frustrating experience.[42]

Active participation in the political processes has not been a characteristic of public library administrators in many instances. The paucity of services and facilities, the poverty of library resources... are the results of the isolation of the public library administrator within the government... administrators have preferred to remain on the edge of the political process, rather than risk public criticism, pressure from other government officials, adverse publicity including critical "letters to the editor", and the possible loss of position.[43]

The library administrator is drawn principally from the managerial and professional groups, and the majority of administrators, like board members, are over fifty years old.[44] Library administrators tend to stay a long time in their positions; they may stay so long that there is little opportunity for younger energies and ideas to be infused into the system.[45]

Library administrators seek to avoid conflict and try to anticipate community demands. For example, they will call for a referendum only when and in the form that could guarantee victory. They are cautious in their policy initiatives and are reluctant to test the boundaries of their influence. While library administrators make the important decisions, they act within a "zone of tolerance" that is imposed on them by the public. They are free to run the library according to their professional desires and beliefs until they exceed the boundaries of this zone, that is, the latitude or area of maneuverability granted, or yielded, to the library administrator by the local community. When administrators stray outside the zone of tolerance, they can come into conflict with values dear to that particular community and may face the likelihood of controversy and opposition.[46]

PUBLIC LIBRARY BUREAUCRACY

Public libraries are bureaucracies. The reasons are set forth by Beverly Lynch:

The bureaucratic elements which critics identify have their sources not in the red tape or pettiness of officials, but in the attempt of the library to control its environment. The elements of bureaucracy emerge from the library's attempt to ensure its efficiency and its competency and from its attempt to minimize the impact of outside influences."[47]

The fundamental premise of bureaucracy, including library bureaucracy, is that library bureaucratic officials "are significantly—though not solely—motivated by their own self-interest."[48] The power of bureaucrats is based primarily on their unrivaled knowledge of the activities of the public service they administer and on their permanency.[49]

Professionalized library bureaucracy is similar to other public bureaucracies. Library bureaucrats tend to be unresponsive to the library's clients because bureaucratic officials give their first loyalty to the institution rather than the individual client.

The motives of experts frequently are misunderstood and assumed to be more sinister than they actually are. . . . In fact, bureaucrats are not power hungry; rather they are professionally motivated to apply expert knowledge, whether or not the society wants the use of that knowledge. Bureaucrats in education and other policy arenas generally do not seek power for its own sake; they seek instead to impose on the public their professional judgments about desirable outcomes— even over the objections of lay persons who do not share their values.[50]

Public libraries are controlled by library administrators rather than by the professional staff,[51] since there is no significant flow of authority from the library administrator to the professional staff. Since the majority of library administrators adhere to a centralized or authoritative decision-making style, almost half of the library professionals and over 90 percent of the nonprofessional staff within the public library are not involved in actual decision making.[52]

Unlike teachers, public librarians still define their interests no differently from library administrators. They have not become militant, and as a result, the power relations at the local public library level have not changed. The impact of the professional staff is quite limited, and professional librarians as a group exercise little influence over library policy. Professional librarians have not succeeded in gaining control of the public library through unionization or collective bargaining, although library administrators' authority may have become more restricted and librarians' formal authority may have increased. The American Library Association is still dominated by library administrators and has never been a force in influencing internal local library policies, since it has not been concerned with librarian welfare issues.[53]

LOCAL INTEREST GROUPS

Within bureaucracies, professionals tend to be more concerned with the opinions of their colleagues in other communities . . . rather than with the attitudes of their clients. Moreover, the norms of professionalization require that decisions be made according to professional standards—which may run contrary to popular opinion.[54]

The result is that public library policy formation is conducted autonomously by specialists who are virtually impervious to pressures from external forces.[55] Public libraries are a policy arena that is not structured to provide access to interest groups. Library board members do not define themselves as politicians. They see themselves as guardians rather than representatives.

The particular pressures upon public libraries are modest. Where there are demands they tend to be for new branch sites and for traditional services. . . . The sentiment of most of the public library's public tends towards apathy and disinterest. No major interest group appears to be either consistently supportive or violently opposed.[56]

No organized group on the local level expresses itself on public library issues. There is no competition among various groups for influence and control in public library governance. There have been few demands for shared control of the public library, even from library users. Groups will seldom get involved in library policy making because they believe that they have no chance to influence policy or because they do not consider library policy significant. Minority groups may challenge the equity of public library service; other groups may challenge material that they consider inappropriate; and taxpayers' associations may challenge major new programs or facilities which may require an increase in the tax rate on the grounds of fiscal responsibility.

Significant pressures are exerted only when the public library has to decide on the location of new library facilities, the closing of library facilities or the curtailment of services in particular locations.

CONCLUSION

The issue of the relative position and relationship between public library board, library administrator, professional library staff, and the public, as well as the viability of the library board, have been considered in the past. Crises in particular communities might have led to changes in the governance of these public libraries, but in general the traditional pattern has been retained.

NOTES

1. Harvey J. Tucker and L. Harmon Zeigler, *The Politics of Educational Governance: An Overview* (Eugene: University of Oregon, ERIC Clearinghouse on Educational Management, 1980), pp. 8–9.

2. Ibid., p. 13.

3. Ibid., p. 21.

4. James D. Koerner, *Who Controls American Education? A Guide to Laymen* (Boston: Beacon Press, 1968), p. 122.

5. Kenneth Prewitt, "Political Ambitions, Volunteerism, and Electoral Accountability," *American Political Science Review* 64 (March 1970): 10.

6. Donald W. Koepp, *Public Library Government: Seven Case Studies* (Berkeley: University of California Press, 1968), pp. 123–130.

7. Morton Kroll, "Public Library Boards of Trustees," in *Public Libraries of the Pacific Northwest*, ed. Morton Kroll (Seattle: University of Washington Press, 1960), pp. 143–144.

8. Ibid., p. 222.

9. S. L. Baker, "A Survey of Illinois Library Trustees," *Illinois Library Statistical Report 14* (Springfield: Illinois State Library, 1984); Margaret A.B. Williams and Bernard S. Schlessinger, "Texas Public Library Trustee," *Public Library Quarterly* 5 (Winter 1984): 41–45; David K. Hamilton, "Citizen Participation in Suburbia: The Library Board," *Illinois Libraries* 64 (September 1982): 955–962; Ann E. Prentice, *The Public Library Trustee: Image and Performance on Funding* (Metuchen, N.J.: Scarecrow Press, 1973).

10. Baker, "A Survey of Illinois Library Trustees"; Williams and Schlessinger, "Texas Public Library Trustee."

11. Ruth Mary Bundy and Paul Wasserman, *The Public Library Administrator and His Situation* (Washington, D.C.: U.S. Office of Education, Bureau of Research, 1970), p. 50.

12. Prentice, *The Public Library Trustee*, pp. 49–51.

13. Kroll, "Public Library Boards of Trustees," p. 139.

14. Prentice, *The Public Library Trustee*, p. 51.

15. Alex Ladenson, *Library Law and Legislation in the United States* (Metuchen, N.J.: Scarecrow Press, 1982), p. 31.

16. Baker, "A Survey of Illinois Library Trustees."

17. Roberta H. Gellert, "Public Library Decision-Making: An Investigation of the Process, the Participants, Power, and Influence." D.L.S. dissertation, Columbia University, 1981.

18. Frank W. Lutz, "Local School Board Decision-Making: A Political-Anthropological Analysis," *Education and Urban Society* 12 (August 1980): 459.

19. Minnie-Lou Lynch, "Organization of the Library Board," in *The Library Trustee: A Practical Guidebook*, 3d ed., ed. Virginia G. Young (New York: Bowker, 1978), pp. 21, 20.

20. Koepp, *Public Library Government*, p. 165.

21. Lynch, "Organization of the Library Board," p. 21.

22. Tucker and Zeigler, *The Politics of Educational Governance*, p. 21.

23. Joseph Pois, "The Board and the General Superintendent," in *Governing Education*, ed. Alan Rosenthal (Garden City, N.Y.: Anchor, 1969), p. 427.

24. Paul E. Peterson, "The Politics of American Education," *Review of Research in Education* 2 (1974): 350.

25. Norman D. Kerr, "The School Board as an Agency of Legitimization," *Sociology Of Education* 38 (Autumn 1964): 34–59.

26. David W. Minar, "Community Characteristics, Conflict, and Power Structures," in *The Politics of Education in the Local Community*, ed. Robert S. Cahill and Stephen P. Hencley (Danville, Ill.: Interstate Printers & Publishers, 1964), p. 141.

27. Jeffrey L. Pressman, "Preconditions of Mayoral Leadership," *American Political Science Review* 66 (June 1972): 515.

28. Young, "The Trustee as Policy Maker," in *The Library Trustee: A Practical Guidebook*, 3d ed., ed. Virginia G. Young (New York: Bowker, 1978), p. 24; Virginia G. Young, *The Trustee of a Small Public Library* (Chicago: ALA, 1978), p. 6.

29. Robert S. Alvarez, "Profile of Public Library Chiefs: A Serious Survey with Some Comic Relief," *Wilson Library Bulletin* 47 (March 1973): 579.

30. Baker, "A Survey of Illinois Library Trustees," p. 16.

31. Ibid.

32. Gellert, "Public Library Decision-Making."

33. Minnie-Lou Lynch, "Organization of the Library Board," p. 20.

34. Virginia G. Young, "The Trustee as Policy Maker," p. 24.

35. Ibid., p. 23.

36. Edward Banfield and James Q. Wilson, *City Politics* (New York: Vintage, 1963), p. 222.

37. Harmon Zeigler, Ellen Kehoe, and Jane Reisman, *City Managers and School Superintendents: Response to Community Conflict* (New York: Praeger, 1985), p. 1.

38. Michael O. Boss et al., "Professionalism, Community Structure, and Decision-Making School Superintendents and Interest Groups," in *Political Science and School Politics: The Princes and the Pundits*, ed. Samuel K. Gove and Frederick M. Wirt (Lexington, Mass.: Lexington Books, 1976), p. 43.

39. Zeigler et al., *City Managers and School Superintendents*, p. 22.

40. Banfield and Wilson, *City Politics*, p. 216.

41. Malcolm Getz, *Public Libraries: An Economic View* (Baltimore: Johns Hopkins University Press, 1980), pp. 153–154.

42. Bundy and Wasserman, *The Public Library Administrator*, p. 18.

43. Phyllis I. Dalton, "The Library and the Political Processes," in *Local Public Library Administration*, ed. Ellen Altman (Chicago: ALA, 1980), p. 31.

44. Bundy and Wasserman, *The Public Library Administrator*, pp. 5-7.

45. Ruth Kay Maloney, "The 'Average' Director of a Large Public Library," *Library Journal* 96 (February 1, 1971): 445.

46. Joseph H. McGivney and William Moynihan, "School and Community," *Teachers College Record* 74 (December 1972): 209–224.

47. Beverly P. Lynch, "Libraries as Bureaucracies," *Library Trends* 27 (Winter 1978): 267.

48. Anthony Downs, *Inside Bureaucracy* (Boston: Little, Brown, 1967), p. 2.

49. Douglas M. Fox, *The Politics of City and State Bureaucracy* (Pacific Palisades, Calif.: Goodyear Publishing, 1974), p. 19.

50. Zeigler et al., *City Managers and School Superintendents*, p. 5.

51. Bundy and Wasserman, *The Public Library Administrator*, pp. 54–55.

52. Jane Robbins, *Citizen Participation and Public Library Policy* (Metuchen, N.J.: Scarecrow Press, 1975), pp. 36, 42.

53. Katherine Todd, "Collective Bargaining and Professional Associations in the Library Field," *Library Quarterly* 55 (July 1985): 284–299.

54. J. Rogers Hollingsworth, "Perspectives on Industrializing Societies," in *Emerging Theoretical Models in Social and Political History*, ed. Allan G. Bogue (Beverly Hills, Calif,: Sage, 1973), p. 111.

55. Tucker and Zeigler, *The Politics of Educational Governance*, p. 21.

56. Bundy and Wasserman, *The Public Library Administrator*, pp. 68.

5

Citizen Participation in Local Public Librarianship

The Advisory Commission on Intergovernmental Relations has stated that

Citizen participation beyond the electoral process ... constitutes a vital complementary feature of contemporary American government, and is essential for holding elected and appointed officials accountable, exerting a salutary influence on governmental decisions, contributing to improved governmental services, and strengthening citizens' confidence in, and support for, government.[1]

Paradoxically, Jane Robbins found that although the American public library has always claimed that its services were available and provided to all persons across the societal spectrum, it was only recently that the democracy of its decision-making processes has been directly scrutinized and challenged.[2]

Citizen participation refers to purposeful activities in which people take part in relation to governmental units of which they are legal residents.[3] Some of the conclusions of the research regarding citizen participation can be summarized as follows:

1. Participation is central to the functioning of a democratic society, but even under the best of conditions most people tend to avoid participation.

2. Low-income citizens participate less than those in higher socio-economic categories, but many of them do participate actively.

3. Groups that do participate can surmount barriers to their participation, but gaining access may not be easy.

4. There is an ever-present force of "potential participation" in every major institution.

5. Localizing control does not necessarily increase participation.

6. Administrative agencies often use participation as an instrument to achieve their own ends without any significant transfer of power.

7. There are strong administrative obstacles to the expansion of participation; official and citizen views of participation tend to be inherently contradictory.[4]

Citizen participation plays a limited role in determining municipal service performance. The quantity and quality of citizen participation in local public library governance are low. Instead of the public determining library policy, it is shaped primarily by professional librarians who enjoy substantial insulation from public opinion and political accountability. Lay influence is nonexistent in most localities, and even when it does exist, it is extremely limited. Individual citizens cannot hold the public library directly responsible for the quality of the services it renders.

Citizens have little influence on the public library decision-making process. In lower-income communities there is a lack of action-directed organizations, coupled with frustration over or disinterest in library issues. The environment of the city's political life and the operating style of the public library do not support or encourage effective citizen participation in major library policy issues. Citizen access to such issues is generally limited, because library administrators control the flow of information about the library. Library policy making is essentially closed to those who actively seek a redistribution of resources throughout the public library.[5] "Even where a library administration professes an inclination towards the utilization of citizen group intelligence, the translation of that inclination into reality is problematical."[6]

Compared to the level of interest in local public education, there is a low level of interest in the public library in the community. The public generally abstains from participation in library affairs and seldom makes demands on the public library. As a result, library administrators rarely have to consider public demands or resort to various tactics to deflect lay opposition to their policies. The public library is nonresponsive to public demands because the public generates few demands. Access to the policy-making apparatus does exist, but the public does not make use of it. The public does not express demands frequently and consistently. One of the reasons for public unresponsiveness is disconnectedness, the fact that the public and the public library are generally detached from each other. Library boards do not serve as a forum to the public for addressing critical issues. On the contrary, important issues are given relatively little time in board meetings, with most attention centered on routine matters.

Public librarians are unwilling to share what they perceive to be their professional prerogatives with the residents of their community. Over 50 percent of librarians have a rather strong negative attitude toward citizen participation; over 70 percent have less than a positive attitude.[7] Library boards apparently agree with the librarians' attitude. "So long as quality services in adequate amounts are delivered on the neighborhood level, the average citizen will be little interested in community control of governmental institutions and functions."[8]

Public libraries have few constituencies, and services provided by the public library do not provide focus for organized lobbies. Public libraries' lack of political clout is the result of not having local, organized constituencies. "If lack of constituencies makes life easier, in emergencies it boomerangs."[9] The impact of this problem becomes clear from a report on the effects of Proposition 13:

Alameda County was the only library system in California to temporarily shut down after the passage of the tax measure.... But the community did not take it quietly. Angry residents stormed Board of

Supervisors meetings, interrupted proceedings and demanded that the libraries be opened. Now libraries are a high priority for the county. "The libraries have created a surprisingly good lobby."[10]

The demands for more citizen participation in local government have come from federal and state government officials (as well as from local residents) through the practice of legislative mandating of citizen participation and requirements for advisory committees and public hearings. These requirements are guided by the belief that citizen participation will lead to better, or at least more accountable, municipal services at the neighborhood level.[11] Some states also encourage citizen participation through open meeting laws.

The "new reform movement" of the 1960s and 1970s challenged the tenets of the municipal reform movement, including professionalism and centralization.

The growing popularity of the concept of community control is a reaction against a professionalized and specialized bureaucracy insulated from influence by citizens and to some extent by elected officials. Consumers of municipal services often resent the patronizing attitude of "expert administrators," and feel that as citizens they have no voice in determining the policy of the administering agency, which appears to be a fiefdom, as the modes of access to the centers of decision making excludes them.[12]

The general public, however, generates few demands. Citizens seldom participate in the public library arena. Jane Robbins found citizen participation in only 5.7 percent of all the decision-making arenas.[13] Most of the citizens who do participate come out to help, not to lobby. Most of the public approves of their libraries and do not consider the absence of lay control as a major issue.

Conflicts between the public and the public library seldom occur, since conflicts only occur when certain conditions exist. In order that a controversy will develop out of an event the following conditions must exist:

1. The event must touch upon an important aspect of the community members' lives.

2. The event must affect the lives of different community members differently.

3. The event must be one about which community members feel that action can be taken.[14]

An example of such a conflict happened in November 1975 when the Queens Borough Public Library, because of budget cutbacks, scheduled the closing of eleven branches. The branches chosen for closure were those that did not "have the numbers"—that is, they had the lowest book circulation figures. There were strong protests by various community organizations and the National Association for the Advancement of Colored People (NAACP) filed a racial discrimination lawsuit in federal court. The protest was due to the fact that eight branches were in predominantly black neighborhoods, and many residents believed that circulation figures were not as important as community service.[15]

With the exception of the concerns of some residents over tax proposals, over what some may consider inappropriate material in the public library, and concerns over the closing of library branches, the conditions for community conflicts regarding public library issues seldom occur.

ADVISORY GROUPS

Citizen involvement in the public library usually takes the form of lay advisory groups. Library administrators dominate the advisory groups through their exercise of three critical gatekeeping functions. Library administrators (1) have a monopoly on information, (2) control the issues to be brought before the advisory group, and (3) can manipulate the alternative recommendations.

Advisory councils are largely made up of traditional supporters of the public library and the status quo: members of the middle class who are susceptible to cooptation by public library officials. "Cooptation is the process by which an administrator brings potential opposition into the decision process. Conflict thus takes place within the decision-making body."[16] Members of the advisory council are generally appointed by the city council or by the library board. Library administrators will work actively to influence the advisory group's composition. Members may also be representatives of minority groups not represented on the library board. Membership on advisory councils is sometimes viewed as "training" for full board membership. Membership, however, is generally an unstable group, having a high turnover rate.

An advisory group can do very little because it lacks clear and concise remit. It also lacks the staff necessary to service it and is dependent on the library administration. It does not have funds of its own. The attitude of library boards toward advisory groups is similar to that of school boards, which was summed up by Robert Jennings in two statements: First, they are an acceptable part of the trappings of good library community relations in today's world. Second, they are the administrator's problem and concern.[17] The library board does not want advisory groups to have any semblance of officiality or to share the legal powers and duties of the board. The public relations function is seen as the councils' best or most usable feature.

Some library administrators see in the advisory council another body that can intrude in the policy decision-making process, as well as in the internal management of the public library.

Inviting citizens' opinions . . . can be a legitimate step toward their full participation. But if consulting them is not combined with other modes of participation, their rung of the ladder is still a sham since it offers no assurance that citizens concerns and ideas will be taken into account.[18]

Friends of the Library is another library group whose role is generally supportive of the public library. Friends of the Library is a citizen organization "that provide the library with money, numerous volunteer services, advocacy, public relations assistance, and community involvement."[19] It is the creation of the library administrator and can be easily controlled by him. Friends of the Library does not exist to articulate demands. The handbook for members specifically states that a friends group will exist only if the library director desires it and that "all those involved must understand that Friends do not make policy."[20] It appeals to a narrow segment of the community, and leaders of the friends are similar to library board members. Roberta Gellert found that Friends of the Library and other such groups connected to public libraries do not play an influential role and have no influence on public library decision making.[21]

Other community and neighborhood organizations, such as block clubs, educational, religious, political, and racial groups as well as taxpayers' organizations, occasionally try to pressure the public library. Only seldom do such groups succeed.

DECENTRALIZATION

Decentralization of public services is seen as an instrument for making bureaucracy more responsive. Those advocating neighborhood governments maintain that such governments would "enable residents to achieve greater self-governance and take major responsibility for managing service delivery and achieving neighborhood wholeness."[22]

Library services in urban areas have always been decentralized. Service to neighborhoods exists in the public library through branches which are established in various neighborhoods of the city. The neighborhood, however, has absolutely no control over the branch or the service. Decision making has always been centralized. Decentralization, involving the establishment of representative community boards at the neighborhood branch level, was never achieved, probably because it was never tried.[23] It must, however, be remembered that there has been little demand for decentralization. Large public libraries have not moved toward administrative decentralization, but neither has there been much advocacy of greater community control of public libraries. Rarely has citizen participation manifested itself regarding control of neighborhood libraries.

ELECTIONS

The usual process of electing public officials is still the most important aspect of citizen participation. Elections for public library boards are conducted in only a small number of public libraries, usually at large rather than by districts. These elections are generally nonpartisan and are held separately from other elections. The effects of these measures have been summarized by Anne Just:

1. They keep voter turnout low and restricted to those who are directly affected by the election—librarians and library users.
2. They depress the level of competition and discourage the rejection of incumbents standing for reelection.
3. They diminish the exposition of differences among candidates.[24]

Furthermore, public library elections are seldom issue oriented.

Nonpartisan Elections

In nonpartisan elections, the candidates for public office, such as library board members, are recruited, selected, and supported by the community's power structure rather than by political parties. Partisan elections increase the mobilization of voters and participation in the political process. They also increase the supply of information to voters on candidates and issues with more focus on issues than on the characteristics of candidates. Boards elected in a nonpartisan manner have a conservative bias; they are oriented toward the maintenance of the status quo, they are socially unresponsive, they favor centralized decision making, and they tend to be dominated by the professional library staff.[25]

Partisan elections result in more competition for office, more demands for policy changes, and more responsiveness to the community. They give voters a clearer view of the different attitudes and opinions of the candidates and their policy positions and provide the voters with a choice among the policy alternatives. Partisan elections would bring the electorate's attention to the fact that library decisions are political decisions.

At-Large Elections

Library boards appointed or elected at large are not representative of all segments of the community. Certain groups in the community are disadvantaged by at-large elections, while district elections give previously underrepresented groups a "voice" in decision making. When public officials, such as library board members, were part of the local political system of the city, they had to be fairly responsive to the demands of citizens because their continuation in this position depended upon a local electorate. At-large elections lose some measure of accountability of such public officials. Voters, however, participate very little in the opportunity to vote on either library board members or policy matters. When voting in board or tax levy elections, citizens are usually uninformed and uninterested.

REFERENDA

Referenda held for or by public libraries are of several types, but the majority are fiscal referenda, involving bond issues and tax levy increases.[26]

A bond-issue referendum is a peculiarly isolated phenomenon because it puts a policy decision squarely on the individual voter.... A bond-issue election provides a possibility for a direct check by the people of the actions of library boards, one of the few ways they have of doing so. Yet, it appears that the electorate... rarely uses that check in a decisive fashion. Library bond issues ordinarily either win or lose by a close margin and, if they fail, are the victims more of apathy than opposition.[27]

Voter turnout in library referenda is usually rather low. There is some evidence that increased turnout of voters in a referendum election is generally associated with the defeat of the referendum. Furthermore, the greater the community's level of organized opposition to the referendum, the more likely is its defeat; low or less intense opposition is generally associated with the success of the referendum. "Individuals with higher education levels and higher-status jobs appear to be more favorably inclined toward public libraries and are more prepared to support them than are individuals with less education and lower-status jobs."[28] The areas of the city that are regarded as better residential neighborhoods are more likely to vote for the library than against it. In areas of middle income, which are low in the number of college-trained persons and high in number of industrial workers, voter turnout will be low.

CONCLUSION

Regardless of its rhetoric, the public library has not been more democratic than other local government bureaucracies. Public participation in public library governance has been negligible.

NOTES

1. Advisory Commission on Intergovernmental Relations, *Citizen Participation in the American Federal Systems* (Washington, D.C.: GPO, 1980), p. 307.

2. Jane Robbins, *Citizen Participation and Public Library Policy* (Metuchen, N.J.: Scarecrow Press, 1975), p. xi.

3. Stuart Langton, "What is Citizen Participation?" in *Citizen Participation in America: Essays on the State of the Art*, ed. Stuart Langton (Lexington, Mass.: Lexington Books, 1978), pp. 16–17.

4. Barry Checkoway and Jon Van Til, "What Do We Know About Citizen Participation? A Selective Review of Research," in *Citizen Participation in America*, pp. 27–34; James A. Riedel, "Citizen Participation: Myths and Realities," *Public Administration Review* 32 (May/June 1972): 212.

5. Marilyn Gittel, *Limits to Citizen Participation* (Beverly Hills, Calif.: Sage, 1980), p. 241.

6. Robbins, *Citizen Participation and Public Library Policy*, pp. 133–134.

7. Ibid., pp. 58–59.

8. Joseph F. Zimmerman, "Neighborhoods and Citizen Involvement," *Public Administration Review* 32 (May/June 1972): 210.

9. Alvin Rabushka and Pauline Ryan, *The Tax Revolt* (Stanford, Calif.: Hoover Institution, 1982), p. 126.

10. Terry Schwadron, ed., *California and the American Tax Revolt: Proposition 13 Five Years Later* (Berkeley: University of California Press, 1984), p. 164.

11. Richard L. Cole, *Citizen Participation and the Urban Policy Process* (Lexington, Mass.: Lexington Books, 1975), p. 7.

12. Joseph F. Zimmerman, "Neighborhoods and Citizen Involvement," *Public Administration Review* 32 (May/June 1972): 202.

13. Robbins, *Citizen Participation and Public Library Policy*, pp. 56–57.

14. James S. Coleman, *Community Conflict* (New York: Free Press, 1957). p. 4. Cf. Paul E. Peterson, *City Limits* (Chicago: University of Chicago Press, 1981), p. 120.

15. *New York Times*, November 2, 1975.

16. Leigh Stelzer, "Institutionalizing Conflict Response: The Case of Schoolboards," *Social Science Quarterly* 55 (September 1974): 381.

17. Robert E. Jennings, "School Advisory Council in America: Frustration and Failure," in *The Politics of School Government*, ed. George Baron (Oxford: Pergamon Press, 1981), pp. 23–51.

18. Sherry R. Arnstein, "A Ladder of Citizen Participation," *Journal of the American Institute of Planners* 35 (July 1969): 216–224.

19. Sandy Dolnick, ed., *Friends of Libraries Sourcebook* (Chicago: ALA, 1980), p. ix.

20. Sandy Dolnick, "What's a Friend For," in *Friends of Libraries Sourcebook*, p. 2.

21. Roberta H. Gellert, "Public Library Decision-Making: An Investigation of the Process, the Participants, Power, and Influence." D.L.S. dissertation, Columbia University, 1981, pp. 294, 311.

22. Howard W. Hallman, *Neighborhoods: Their Place in Urban Life* (Beverly Hills, Calif.: Sage, 1984), p. 267.

23. Mary Lee Bundy, "Urban Information and Public Libraries: A Design for Service," *Library Journal* 97 (January 15, 1972): 169.

24. Anne E. Just, "Urban School Board Elections," *Education and Urban Society* 4 (August 1980): 421–435.

25. Valerie Nilesen and Norman Robinson, "Partisan School Board Elections: New Evidence to Support the Case for Them," *Administrator's Notebook* 29, no. 3 (1980–81): 1–4.

26. Ruth G. Lindahl and William S. Berner, *Financing Public Library Expansion: Case Studies of Three Defeated Bond Issue Referenda* (Springfield: Illinois State Library, 1968).

27. Guy Garrison, "Voting on a Library Bond Issue: Two Elections in Akron, Ohio, 1961 and 1962," *Library Quarterly* 33 (July 1963): 229.

28. Lawrence J. White, *The Public Library in the 1980s: The Problems of Choice* (Lexington, Mass.: Lexington Books, 1983), p. 56.

6

The Politics of Public Library Fragmentation and Consolidation

THE LARGER LIBRARY UNIT

The reform theory of municipal government assumed that because local government is fragmented, it is also inefficient, ineffective, unresponsive, and uncoordinated.[1] The reform movement has devoted itself to getting rid of separately incorporated and fragmented governments, considering the multiplication of governments to cause parochialism, to provide differing levels of public service, to fragment the tax base into competing jurisdictions, and to result in wasteful duplication and fiscal disparity between public libraries. The solution that library leaders have proposed for this situation follows that proposed by reformers of local government. That solution emphasizes the need to establish large library units, funded by and providing library service to an area larger than one municipality through the consolidation of small public libraries.

Since the publication of Carleton Joeckel's *Government of the American Public Library* in 1934,[2] "the validity of the system concept has been virtually unquestioned in the library profession," and the idea was accepted by successive professional leaders without controversy.[3] Statements regarding the larger library unit have been asserted for so long that they are assumed to be true. It has become conventional wisdom that larger library administrative units are more effective and more efficient in all crucial aspects than smaller ones.

The assumption that small public libraries are inefficient and are unable to provide effective library service or the resources available from larger public libraries has been widely accepted as a library dogma. This dogma has continuously supported the merits of the larger library unit. *The National Plan for Public Library Service* of 1948 called for large public library units, each having a population of about 90,000 and an area of 2,500 square miles.[4] Although the American Library Association avoided defining the larger library unit, it suggested in 1956 that such a unit should have a minimum population of 150,000.[5]

Underlying the case for larger administrative library units is the belief that well-trained professional library administrators are needed to control and direct public library operations. The municipal reform movement has emphasized this kind of professionalism and centralization of executive authority. Library reformers, aware that most small public libraries were not administered by professional librarians, saw in the consolidation of small public libraries into larger units a way of bringing about the professionalization of public librarianship. Also following the conclusions reached by public administrators, they believed that large public libraries would provide more effective and efficient library service through the realization of economies of scale. Economies of scale refer to a group of phenomena that usually cause average costs of a public service to fall as the size of the governmental unit providing this service increases. Library reformers also predicted that large public libraries, because of their size, would be more visible. As a result of such visibility, they would be more responsive to public needs. Consolidation of small public libraries into larger units was also a way of getting rid of what library leaders considered as parochialism in small public libraries. Library leaders wished to follow in the footsteps of school administrators, who, using similar rationale, had succeeded in reducing significantly the number of school districts.[6]

The wholesale consolidation of small public libraries into

larger units did not materialize. Local public libraries did not want to give up their autonomy. The legislation and funds available to school administrators to force small school districts to consolidate were not available to library administrators. Oliver Garceau commented in 1949 about

the stubborn resistance of librarians, boards, and local governments to any deadlines for larger units of service. Postponement and compromise have already set in. Even lavish grants have not disciplined the profession, persuaded the local governments, or impressed the friends of local libraries.[7]

Instead of realizing a small number of larger public libraries, the opposite occurred. Between 1951 and 1984, many small public libraries were established, and the number of public libraries increased from 6,416 to 8,796. In 1982, 64 percent of all public libraries served a population of less than 10,000, and 81 percent served a population of less than 25,000.[8] While the number of medium-sized public libraries (serving populations between 25,000 and 100,000) increased from 633 in 1960 to 1,253 in 1982, their percentage of total public libraries decreased during that period from 16.1 percent to 14.5 percent.[9]

The larger unit was not achieved in many places for a number of reasons. The majority of citizens felt that consolidation results in excessive centralization of political power, loss of community identity, and higher taxes, without a concomitant improvement in the quality of public services. When given the opportunity, voters generally reject consolidation. Nationwide, movements for more centralized local governmental units have been rejected by voters nearly three times as often as they have been passed. A 1973 nationwide survey clearly demonstrated that citizen confidence in local government increases as the size of the governmental unit decreases.[10] Similarly, suburbanites believe that residents of smaller communities are more likely to have access to their governments and to have more influence on political decision making. As a result, about a quarter of the metropolitan inhabitants reside in municipalities, towns, or townships with less than 25,000 population. Most of them are suburban, but some are enclave cities surrounded by the central city.[11] Many of these local governmental units have an independent public library.

Even though there was consensus among library leaders about its advantages, the trend toward consolidation did not materialize because local residents wanted to control their own public library. While residents were unable to prevent school consolidation, since the offer of money by the state to achieve such consolidation was too powerful to resist, they could retain their local public library, and most of them did.

There are no empirical studies to support the assertion that small public libraries are not viable. The dominant conception of library professional leadership as to how public libraries should be organized precluded even considering such a possibility. This dominant conception of the public library has been stated in the various standards for public library service issued by the American Library Association. Indeed, the title of the these standards (*Minimum Standards for Public Library Systems*) precluded any other interpretation.

Consolidation of small public libraries and the larger library unit did not produce the much-sought economies of scale. The assumption that increase in size will improve the public library's performance and lower its costs has been the conventional wisdom, but no evidence supports the proposition that larger size is related to lower costs.[12] There are few economies of scale in moving from a small to a medium-sized public library, but significant diseconomies of scale are likely to accrue in large public libraries. There is no evidence that large public libraries provide better service than small or medium-sized libraries. The opposite may be true. No economies of scale were found for a labor-intensive service, such as the public library, for jurisdictions beyond the size of 15,000 to 20,000. In cities over 250,000 population, size does make a difference, and there are significant diseconomies of scale.[13] The conditions that help private industry to benefit from scale economies simply do not appear to exist when local urban governments consolidate.

The expectations for economy and efficiency have been seldom realized. Although the conditions under which economies of scale might be realized are present in many reformed metropolitan institutions, there is little evidence that they are

Table 10
Per Capita Amounts Spent by Public Libraries, by Size of
Population, 1982

Population Size	Per Capita Amount
Total	8.23
1,000,000 or more	11.47
500,000 to 999,999	11.03
250,000 to 499,999	8.33
100,000 to 249,999	7.55
50,000 to 99,999	5.14
25,000 to 49,999	4.46
10,000 to 24,999	4.15
Less than 9,999	3.82

Source: U.S. Bureau of the Census, 1982 Census of Governments, Vol. 4: Governmental Finances, No. 5: Compendium of Government Finances (Washington, DC.: GPO, 1984), Table 49.

being realized. Smaller public libraries are just as capable as large public libraries of achieving economies of scale, and they are more efficient than large public libraries. The larger the population served by the public library, the larger the per capita amount spent by the public library (Table 10).

When performance levels of larger public library rise, so do the library's expenditure and the resulting fiscal burden that it lays on local residents. A greater number of public library employees results only in a higher perception of quality in the provision of public library service.[14]

CONSOLIDATION

The assignment of public library service to a local government is a matter of historical development and political choice. Public library service is shared among all types of local governments, but municipalities have always been the dominant provider. Criteria for the assignment of library service to a specific local government unit have been seldom formulated or utilized.

In 1974 the Advisory Commission on Intergovernmental Relations attempted to formulate a rational basis for assigning or placing functional responsibilities among the various governmental units. The guidelines called for the placement of a function in the jurisdiction that can provide that service:

1. Most economically, for example, providing library service at the lowest possible cost.
2. Most equitably, having an adequate fiscal capacity and effective performance.
3. Most effectively, having an effective legal and jurisdictional authority and administrative capability to perform the service assigned to it.
4. With adequate political responsibility, maximizing the conditions for active citizen participation while still permitting adequate performance, that is, control by and accessibility to those served, and offering maximum opportunity for active citizen participation.[15]

Numerous proposals have been made over the years for reorganizing governments, particularly governments of metropolitan areas. These range from minor changes, such as intergovernmental agreements, transfer of functions, and special districts, to radical changes, such as consolidation of cities and counties. All such reorganizations must generally follow a decision by the governmental units involved and their ratification in a voter referendum.[16]

The simplest, most common, and most successful method of increasing the population served by a municipal public library is through annexation, enlarging the municipality's limits into unincorporated territory not part of another municipality. Proposals for metropolitan or city-county consolidations, on the other hand, have seldom been successful, because the consolidation of independent local government units is not an administrative matter, but rather a politically difficult endeavor. Suburban residents strongly oppose solving metropolitan problems by consolidating their local governments with the government of the core city. As a result, most proposals for governmental consolidation meet stiff resistance. Between the end of World War II and 1976, seventeen city-county consolidations have been achieved out of eighty-six attempts, sometimes through legislatively mandated merger. Only three involved more than 250,000 people: Nashville–Davidson County in 1962, Jacksonville–Duval County in 1967, and Indianapolis–Marion County in 1969. In these consolidated units, the public library was consolidated as well. Even these libraries may not provide service to all the residents of the consolidated unit, and independent public libraries may remain within their jurisdictions. Indianapolis and Marion County, Indiana, were incorporated by order of the state legislature, and a consolidated public library was created, but two communities still retain their independent public libraries.

While complete city-county consolidation has seldom been achieved, the consolidation of library service between city and county has been much more successful. When the city transfers its public library to the county, a metropolitan public library is created. In other situations, the urban county, outside the limits of the core city, may provide consolidated public library service. City and county may enter an agreement under which the city or the county assumes responsibility for public library service. The urban county public library is a compromise of providing library service without political integration. In 1971 the Miami–Dade Public Library System took over public library service in the city and the county (through the device of a special taxing district), serving seventeen cities within the county as well as the unincorporated area. Nine small cities, however, did not join the county library and still retain their own public libraries. Out of 291 metropolitan counties responding to a questionnaire in 1975, 217 (74 percent) provided library service.[17]

Regional or metropolitan library districts are established pursuant to local referenda and are governed by local appointees. They may serve all or a substantial part of the metropolitan area. The regional library district may also be created by state law and removed from local control. Regional library districts are created for a variety of economic and political reasons, but many of them are characterized by a general lack of accessibility, political accountability, and public control. Regional library districts may also be established as a result of a contract between two or more counties, as is the case in Kentucky. The library board is appointed by a joint action of the county boards of the member counties.

INTERGOVERNMENTAL AGREEMENTS

Suburban governments wishing to preserve themselves and at the same time provide public library service have followed a variety of strategies. Contracting between local governmental units as a means for providing library service has been a common practice. A local government may enter into an agreement with another local government for the provision of public library service to its citizens by the other local government. An intergovernmental service agreement allows a local government to obtain public library service for its citizens, which it cannot provide itself or which it is unwilling to provide. Contracts have been entered into between a county and municipalities, between two or more counties, or between one municipality and another.

Public libraries have been one of the top five activities involved in service agreements, and both formal or informal service agreements between local governments for the provision of public library service have been popular. In 1972 there were some 350 intergovernmental service agreements, either formal or informal, for the provision of public library service.[18] Service agreements are flexible as to their duration and the territory that the service will cover. Public library service agreements are used primarily because local governments believe that these agreements will take advantage of economies of scale.[19] Local governments believe that they will be able to lower the costs and improve the quality of library service by obtaining it from another governmental unit. Service agreements are politically feasible because they do not require changes in the basic governmental structure of the participating localities. States may also provide the legal framework for such agreements.

Joint service agreements for the provision of public library service occur when two or more governmental units join forces to provide this service. Charlotte and Mecklenburg County,

North Carolina, have such a joint public library service agreement. A joint body is usually established to administer the service. Costs of the service are allocated between the participating jurisdictions, but some joint agreements have been terminated because of disputes over the apportionment of costs.

While library service may be the only service to be contracted, it can also be one of a package of services contracted by one jurisdiction from another. The "Lakewood Plan" in Los Angeles County is the most significant of such plans. Under this plan, municipalities contract with the County of Los Angeles for a wide range of public services. Of the eighty-four municipalities in Los Angeles County which have service agreements with the county, forty-eight municipalities have contracted for public library service. Local jurisdictions pay the county for library service through taxes collected by special tax districts.[20] While contract cities have nominal control over service level, they are unable to establish independent service policy. A city cannot always withdraw from the contract system even if it wants to.

Under the contract arrangement . . . [communities] give up a significant measure of independence in return for what they perceive as the values to be derived from participation. Ultimately, the only considerations of importance in the policy making process become those connected with preservation of the system. System-maintenance criteria replace other, more appropriate standards in determining governmental action.[21]

The most important adverse effect of service agreements is a political one. Service agreements place severe limitations on the independence of action of the local community, restrict their freedom of action, and make the public service less responsive to the citizens.

TRANSFER OF FUNCTION

Public library function has been transferred from one local governmental unit to another as an adjustment of the established structure of local government. The majority of transfers have been from municipalities to counties. Larger municipalities generally have greater propensity to transfer functional responsibility than smaller ones. Cities, particularly core cities, have been willing to transfer their responsibility for public library service to urban counties, since certain library services of the core city are also used by residents of the suburbs at no charge, and there is a spillover of library service from the core city to the suburbs. "Suburban residents are often able to consume services in the core city without enduring any financial obligation to support the provision of these services."[22] Studies of spillovers found a high rate of use of the core city public library by nonresidents of that city.[23] One of the stated goals of metropolitan reform has been the capturing of spillovers of governments in the metropolitan area. Some cities have been able to convince the county to take over library service in order to enlarge the tax base for the public library support. Suburban communities with independent public libraries will have to agree, or will be coerced into, giving up their libraries in order to become a part of the county library.

Analysis of metropolitan institutions, however, has shown that much of the expectation for capturing spillovers seldom materializes. A more politically feasible solution to date has been payment by the county or the state to the core city public library for its use by nonresidents.

LIBRARY SYSTEMS

When the consolidation of small libraries into larger units did not materialize on the scale envisioned, library leaders pushed forward with the idea of achieving larger library units through cooperative library systems. In his summary of the Public Library Inquiry, Robert Leigh recommended:

A major direction for public library development ... in line with the official objectives, is the organization of public library systems and concentration of state and Federal financial aid on the encouragement and partial support of such systems.... If public libraries are to approach the objectives of service laid down by their leaders there needs be some participation by the state in their financial support.[24]

Library systems came, therefore, as a result of pressure from single-minded activists in state library associations leadership who in cooperation with the state library agencies, succeeded in pushing library system legislation through state legislatures. Many state library agencies have made the development of library systems a major priority. There was rarely any grassroots demand for the systems from the local public libraries. Only recently have objections to regional library systems become articulated.

A cooperative library system is an organization created and governed by two or more authorities operating their own libraries. Each participating authority continues to operate its library.[25] Cooperative library systems could be achieved only with state funding. State funds were necessary to establish and to maintain library systems. State aid to public libraries was used by the state library agency to encourage or coerce public libraries to join library systems. Public libraries had to join a library system before they become eligible for state aid.

State library agencies have generally taken the position that the objectives of providing basic library service to all the state residents can be achieved by regional cooperation and by cooperative library systems. The states, however, have seldom dictated the size or the boundaries of library systems. Making public library service a compulsory service through legislative fiat, as was done in Great Britain in 1964, is considered politically unfeasible and has not been tried as a solution to achieving this objective.

State library agencies have transferred to the cooperative library systems certain tasks and services, particularly consulting services, previously provided by the state library agency.

FRAGMENTATION

The doctrines of public and business administration which evolved in the first part of this century dictated centralized administration. The metropolitan reform movement gave the centralization of public services a high priority and has devoted itself to ridding metropolitan areas of "fragmented governments." Reformed metropolitan public services would also strengthen the influence of professionals in public policy making. The idea of decentralized administration under neighborhood control, the demands to decentralize bureaucracy and the establishment of community control over public services are contrary to the basic concepts of centralization.

Centralization, however, threatens certain social and political values. Public library service is considered one of the most local services. As a public service that is provided in person-to-person situations, it is sensitive to individual preferences. While the fragmentation of many metropolitan areas into many small governmental units and independent public libraries has been criticized, one can still find many highly fragmented metropolitan areas. The number of public libraries in urban counties varies considerably from place to place. Cook County, Illinois, for example, contains ninety-five independent public libraries, in addition to the Chicago Public Library. A comparison of the library expenditure of the Chicago Public Library with library expenditure in other municipal public libraries within the Chicago Metropolitan Area shows that the majority of suburbs had a higher, and some much higher, per capita expenditure than the central city public library (Table 11).

Branch libraries of a municipal public library may be greatly inferior to independent municipal libraries serving similar populations. Furthermore, fragmentation does not appear to increase or decrease government spending.[26] There are conflicting values and needs among residents and subcommunities in the metropolitan environment. There exists survey evidence that indicates which citizens are in fact more satisfied with smaller units of government.[27] Citizens in smaller communities generally have higher levels of satisfaction with local government services than those in larger communities. Indeed, citizens express preferences for increased fragmentation rather than consolidation, an expression that flies in the face of centralization principles.

There has also been a group of economists and political scientists who justify the existing fragmented system, who apply

Table 11

Per Capita General Expenditure for Public Libraries in the Chicago
Metropolitan Area, 1983–84

Library	Population	Per Capita Expenditure
Arlington Heights	66,116	$ 42.23
Aurora	81,293	12.10
Chicago	3,005,072	10.66
Cicero	61,232	8.07
Des Plaines	55,374	23.77
Elgin	75,136	16.77
Evanston	73,706	20.82
Mount Prospect	52,634	22.36
Niles	52,139	19.65
Oak Lawn	60,590	24.45
Oak Park	54,887	22.40
Palatine*	61,014	16.95
Schaumburg	103,920	20.93
Skokie	60,278	32.59
Waukegan	67,653	24.42

Note: Includes public libraries serving a population of 50,000 or
more.

*Statistics for 1982–1983.

Source: "Illinois Public Library Statistics 1983–1984,"
Illinois Libraries 66 (November 1984): 452–484.

economic reasoning to public service problems, and who equate
the governmental service to a market system in which local
governments provide different types and qualities of services.
An individual can move to the local jurisdiction providing the
mix of services that will benefit that individual the most. "Citizen demands can be more precisely indicated in smaller units
rather than larger political units, and in political units un-
dertaking fewer rather than more numerous public functions."[28]

CONCLUSION

The concept of a larger public library unit succeeded only on a modest scale. This concept as well as the concept of library systems are being questioned today. The opposing concept of decentralization of public library service may gain more momentum in the future.

NOTES

1. Committee for Economic Development, *Modernizing Local Government to Secure a Balanced Federalism* (New York: CED, 1966).

2. Carleton B. Joeckel, *Government of the American Public Library* (Chicago: University of Chicago Press, 1934).

3. Nelson Associates, *Public Library Systems in the United States* (Chicago: ALA, 1969), p. 15; Ruth W. Gregory and Lester L. Stoffel, *Public Libraries in Cooperative Systems: Administrative Patterns for Service* (Chicago: ALA, 1971), pp. 3–5.

4. Carleton B. Joeckel and Amy Winslow, *A National Plan for Public Library Service* (Chicago: ALA, 1948), p. 50.

5. *Public Library Service: A Guide to Evaluation, with Minimum Standards* (Chicago: ALA, 1956), p. 7.

6. Jonathan P. Sher and Rachel B. Tompkins, "Economy, Efficiency, and Equality: The Myths of Rural School and District Consolidation," in *Education in Rural America: A Reassessment of Conventional Wisdom*, ed. Jonathan P. Sher (Boulder, Colo.: Westview, 1977), pp. 43-77.

7. Oliver Garceau, *The Public Library in the Political Process* (New York: Columbia University Press, 1949), pp. 217.

8. *American Library Directory*, 19th ed. (New York: Bowker, 1951); 37th ed. (New York: Bowker, 1984); "An NCLIS Library Statistical Sampler," *Library Journal* 110 (October 15, 1985): 36.

9. Leon Carnovsky, "The Medium-Sized Public Library: In Retrospect and Prospect," *Library Quarterly* 33 (January 1963): 129; "An NCLIS Library Statistical Sampler," p. 36.

10. U.S. Congress, Senate, Committee on Governmental Relations, Subcommittee on Intergovernmental Relations, *Confidence and Concern: Citizens View Americans and Government* (Washington, D.C.: GPO, 1973).

11. Howard W. Hallman, *Neighborhoods: Their Place in Urban Life* (Beverly Hills, Calif.: Sage, 1984), p. 240.

12. Michael D. Cooper, "The Economics of Library Size: A Preliminary Inquiry," *Library Trends* 28 (Summer 1979):63-78.

13. Advisory Commission on Intergovernmental Relations, *Size Can Make a Difference: A Closer Look* (Washington, D.C.: GPO, 1970), p. 2.

14. James A. Christenson and Carolyn E. Sachs, "The Impact of Size of Government and Number of Administrative Units on the Quality of Community Services," *Administrative Science Quarterly* 25 (1980): 99–100.

15. Advisory Commission on Intergovernmental Relations, *Substate Regionalism and the Federal System: Vol. IV, Governmental Functions and Processes: Local and Areawide* (Washington, D.C.: GPO, 1974), pp. 7–8.

16. Thomas M. Scott, "Metropolitan Governmental Reorganization Proposals," *Western Political Quarterly* 21 (June 1968): 252-261.

17. Carolyn B. Lawrence and John M. DeGrock, "County Government Services," *The County Year Book 1976*, p. 98.

18. Advisory Commission on Intergovernmental Relations, *Substate Regionalism and the Federal System: Vol. IV*, p. 33.

19. Advisory Commission on Intergovernmental Relations, *Substate Regionalism and the Federal System: Vol. III: The Challenge of Local Governmental Reorganization* (Washington, D.C.: GPO, 1974), p. 39.

20. Richard M. Cion, "The Lakewood Plan," in *Readings in State and Local Government*, ed. Irwin N. Gertzog (Englewood Cliff, N.J.: Prentice-Hall, 1970), pp. 43–53.

21. Ibid., pp. 48–49.

22. A. G. Holtman, T. Tabasz, and W. Kruse, "The Demand for Local Public Services: Spillovers, and Urban Decay: The Case for Public Libraries," *Public Finance Quarterly* 4 (January 1976): 98.

23. Joseph S. Slavet, Katherine L. Bradbury, and Philip I. Moss, *Financing State-Local Services: A New Strategy for Greater Equity* (Lexington, Mass.: Lexington Books, 1975), pp. 69-71.

24. Robert D. Leigh, *The Public Library in the United States* (New York: Columbia University Press, 1950), pp. 227, 229.

25. Robert R. McClaren, "State Legislation Relating to Library Systems," *Library Trends* 18 (October 1970): 238.

26. Brett W. Hawkins and Thomas R. Dye, "Metropolitan 'Fragmentation': A Research Note," in *Politics in the Metropolis*, 2d ed., ed.

Thomas R. Dye and Brett W. Hawkins (Columbus, Ohio: Merrill, 1971), p. 499.

27. Thomas J. DiLorenzo, "Special Districts and Local Public Services," *Public Finance Quarterly* 9 (July 1981): 359.

28. Robert L. Bish and Vincent Ostrom, *Understanding Urban Government: Metropolitan Reform Reconsidered* (Washington, D.C.: American Enterprise Institute for Public Policy, 1973), p. 24.

7

The Politics of Public Librarianship at the State Level

Public library service is a state function. The state has the legal responsibility for public library service, and the legal basis for operating public libraries is found in the laws of each state. Authority for public libraries stems from the "reserved" power in the U.S. Constitution. The Tenth Amendment to the Constitution reserves to the states those powers not expressly given to the national government nor denied to state governments. As a result, public library service is a state authority, which is, however, administered locally.

Since World War II, state governments have been revitalized and transformed by a "quiet revolution ... into a solid instrument for meeting the complex needs of American society today."[1] As the power and presence of state governments in the federal system increased, and as their capacity to govern and their sensitivity to public needs improved, so did the importance of the state's role in public librarianship.

The reformers' belief that the modernization and democratization of government would put a dent in society's needs seems reasonable. But it appears that the opposite has happened in many states. Needs, programs, special interests, expenditures, rules, and central activities have all multiplied—out of control, some say. Instead of filling the

Table 12

Per Capita Direct General Expenditure of State and Local
Governments for Libraries, by State, 1982–83

State	Expenditure	State	Expenditure
Alaska	31.21	South Dakota	8.41
Wyoming	17.74	Ohio	8.24
Washington	17.53	Montana	8.08
New York	14.49	Missouri	7.99
Connecticut	14.37	Michigan	7.90
Maryland	14.29	Nebraska	7.62
Hawaii	13.69	Alabama	7.32
Iowa	13.04	Kansas	7.26
Wisconsin	13.02	Vermont	6.94
Massachusetts	12.49	Texas	6.89
Utah	11.94	West Virginia	6.89
New Jersey	11.47	Delaware	6.60
Minnesota	11.28	Maine	6.55
California	11.09	Louisiana	6.37
Illinois	10.80	Idaho	6.28
Colorado	10.59	North Carolina	6.03
Nevada	10.18	North Dakota	5.71
Virginia	9.99	Oklahoma	5.39
Florida	9.78	South Carolina	5.39
Oregon	9.86	Kentucky	5.11
Rhode Island	9.59	Pennsylvania	5.00
New Hampshire	9.29	Tennessee	4.92
Arizona	9.26	Mississippi	4.17
Indiana	8.93	Georgia	3.77
New Mexico	8.90	Arkansas	3.42

Source: U.S. Bureau of the Census, Governmental Finances
         1982-83 (Washington, D.C.: GPO, 1984), Table 24.

reservoir of need, progressive state governments appear to have
opened the floodgates of possibilities.[2]

Many state governments continue as direct library service
providers. While only two states are dominant library service
providers (accounting for more than 55 percent of the direct
general expenditure), eighteen states are significant library
service providers (accounting for 15 percent or more of direct
general expenditure).[3]

The role of state government in public librarianship varies
from state to state, since states vary in their governmental
structure and political processes, party structure, political participation, urbanization, industrialization, wealth, and education. The differences between the states may be perceived
from the comparison of the amount of money each state is
willing to spend on its public libraries (Table 12) and from a

Table 13

State Percentage of State and Local Governments' General
Expenditure for Libraries, by State, 1982–83

State	Percentage	State	Percentage
Hawaii	100.0	Nevada	9.9
Kentucky	39.5	Connecticut	9.3
Vermont	38.9	South Carolina	9.1
Alaska	28.0	Michigan	8.8
South Dakota	25.4	North Carolina	8.5
Maine	24.0	Virginia	7.9
North Dakota	23.0	Oregon	6.9
New York	20.3	New Jersey	6.5
Arkansas	20.0	Tennessee	6.5
Utah	19.7	Georgia	6.0
Idaho	19.4	Pennsylvania	5.2
Alabama	18.6	Ohio	5.0
Oklahoma	18.0	Texas	4.8
Delaware	17.5	Illinois	4.8
Mississippi	16.7	Kansas	4.5
West Virginia	16.3	Maryland	4.1
New Mexico	16.0	Iowa	4.0
New Hampshire	14.6	Indiana	3.5
Montana	13.6	Wisconsin	2.7
Louisiana	13.4	California	2.5
Nebraska	12.3	Colorado	1.8
Arizona	12.0	Missouri	1.8
Wyoming	11.0	Florida	1.7
Rhode Island	10.9	Massachusetts	1.5
Washington	10.6	Minnesota	0.0

Source: Calculated from U.S. Bureau of the Census, Governmental
Finances in 1982-83 (Washington, D.C.: GPO, 1984),
Table 13.

comparison of state expenditure as a percentage of state and
local governments' expenditure for public libraries (Table 13).

Noneconomic explanations of state policy are often stronger
than economic explanations. Underlying the interstate variations in state and local control is the state's political culture.
"Political culture may be regarded as an enduring set of publicly shared and socially communicated beliefs, values, and
traditions about politics which constitutes a general framework
of plans, recipes, rules, and institutions for the conduct of political life, especially who gets what, when, and how."[4] Political
culture gives an identity and provides a meaning to political
systems and processes and helps to account for the major differences between states. It affects public perceptions about the
efficiency, ability, and competence of state governments to pursue their responsibilities, the degree of state control, whether

it will expand, and whether local officials will try to evade state influence. Political culture tries to answer such questions as: what should government do, how should it be structured, and who should participate in it? Each of the states is dominated by one of three political subcultures, or a combination thereof.

The *moralistic political subculture* views government as a means for achieving the public good. All citizens are expected to participate in policy making, initiating policies which are in the public interest. The bureaucracy, which administers these policies, is viewed positively as a nonpartisan institution having high ethical principles. The *individualistic political subculture* views government as a marketplace, primarily promoting economic development and initiating only those policies demanded by public opinion. Only professional politicians participate in policy making, and the bureaucracy is considered an undesirable institution. The *traditionalistic political subculture* views government's main function as maintaining the existing order. Policies should be initiated only if they serve the interests of the governing elites, who are the policy makers and who control the bureaucracy.[5]

The purposes of state action in public librarianship are to: (1) stimulate public librarianship through state aid; (2) regulate them through certification, imposition of standards, and requirements on reporting; (3) perform research and collect statistical data, and make the results available; and (4) provide technical assistance and consultants.

STATE CENTRALIZATION

The issue of the value of local control is central to the political conflict concerning the proper role of the state. In the past, the localistic tradition in the provision of public library service has helped to restrict the scope of state government activities and the state's centralistic tendencies in this area. State library agencies could try to persuade local public libraries to adopt state policies and standards or to provide library services favored by the state, but state library agencies seldom required public libraries to follow the state's standards in this area. State library officials deferred to local judgments and seldom asserted a substantial state leadership role in public librarianship. In the last twenty years, the state role has expanded, and public librarianship is becoming increasingly centralized. The power of local control has declined substantially, and local responsibilities and discretion have been eroded.

The impact of federal grants-in-aid was especially significant in enhancing the states' role. Federal statutes and regulations provide for a management role for the states. LSCA specified a role for the states in the administration of the programs under the act. As a result of controlling federal funds on the state level along with their disbursement to local public libraries, the state library agency became "a major arbiter in the success and scope of local libraries."[6]

Provision of more state aid to public libraries is another significant factor in the increase of state centralization and heightens the tension between state and local control. The increase in state control comes into conflict with the passion for local control and the objections of localists to greater state control. However, the "states remain the architects and empowerers of local governments within their boundaries with substantially undiminished control."[7] Still, state library agency officials depend upon local library administrators to implement state programs. Local library administrators are called upon to assist the state library agency in achieving its goals and for assistance in keeping state legislators informed on library matters.

Kenneth Beasley summarized this issue as follows:

The real centralization has come from the increased direct ties of the state library to the local political units in the state and other politically oriented state agencies. In relationship to local government, the state library has been an agent of gross centralization but under a guise of local self-determination. Increased state grants in aid have provided a base for this move, but much more important has been the added federal funds and the recodification of state laws. In tune with the general trend to enlarge the power of state agencies the major characteristic of the recodifications were broader authority for state libraries to promote, develop, and supervise library service for the entire state. At the same time, coercive power was kept to a minimum, usually through the process of allocating state and federal aid and by

setting standards for establishing new libraries and joining systems
and certifying professional employees. However, with a very few exceptions, the latter kind of direct authority has rarely been used as a
major device to *direct* development—it has more often than not followed or reflected development.[8]

STATE POWER STRUCTURE

State power structures exist for decision making in public
librarianship. From among the several types of existing state
power structure, two types can be postulated to be relevant to
public librarianship on the state level. One, the *locally based
disparate structure*, is a loose, weak confederation of public
library administrators of independent local public libraries.
These library leaders interact with legislators from their districts, but they unite only for short periods of time to deal with
significant matters of library policy. In the other type of power
structure, the *statewide monolithic*, state library policy is dominated by an elite group of public library leaders. This group
may be the result of a coalition of the state library groups, often
dominated by the library association, as well as the state library agency. There is seldom competition between these library groups.[9]

STATE LIBRARY POLICIES

Public librarianship at the state level operates in a more
political environment than that at the local level. Partisan
politics and political bargaining are more important at the
state level, because elected state officials tend to be more partisan than local officials. There is greater political competition
between groups in the state political arena.[10]

Public librarianship in most states and in most situations is
not yet a political issue, and is still in the stage of consensus
politics. Public librarianship is dominated by a small group of
professional librarians, mostly library administrators from the
larger public libraries and public library systems. There is
seldom competition between the various state library groups.

On the state level library policy is a peripheral subject. It is seldom dealt with by the state executive or the state legislature (and almost never by the state judiciary). "Few of the basic state laws underpinning the development of public libraries reflect a strong legislative or administrative commitment to insure the establishment of an adequate statewide pattern of library services."[11] Library policies are seldom significant, but they are also seldom controversial, and there is little public conflict about them. Library programs have low visibility. Even in those states that still have a large population unserved by a public library, attention is seldom called to this situation. One of the most important reasons for this state of affairs is that the amount of money involved is extremely small. State expenditures for libraries in fiscal year 1982, including expenditures for the state library agency, totaled $354,312,000, or 0.11 percent of all state governmental expenditures.[12]

Douglas St. Angelo and associates found a high correlation between the political activity of the state library agency and quality library programs and funding. "Combined success on funding and quality state library programs require political activity from the state library professionals and related groups."[13] Library policy is made in three arenas at the state level: the legislature, the governor's office, and the state library agency. In some states the voters themselves participate in policy making through the referendum process. While statewide referenda seldom involve public libraries directly, tax referenda, such as Proposition 13 in California, a state constitutional initiative that limited property taxes, as well as referenda on other subjects, can have a substantial impact on public libraries.

States achieve their goals in public librarianship through financing, regulating, and managing. They provide state aid to local public libraries and mandate certain actions and activities on the part of these local libraries. States change policy through statutes and regulations. Public librarians and state library associations attempt to influence such legislation in order to obtain laws that would be beneficial to public libraries and to prevent laws that would be detrimental to them.

State Legislatures

Following the reapportionment of state legislatures to comply with the "one man, one vote" rule and the legislative reform movement of the 1960s, state legislatures have become more effective and more professional bodies. They are now better apportioned, giving increased voice to urban and suburban interests. Because state legislatures are now representative of all citizens equally, follow democratic practices, and are better staffed, groups can turn to a legislative body that is ready and willing to act. State legislatures can respond more effectively to the needs of their citizens. While the changes have been uneven and some states have participated only slightly, the overall pattern is in the direction of greater professionalism, increased openness, enhanced representativeness, and improved efficiency. State legislatures are still primarily political bodies subject to increasing demands from various groups. In many states, library legislation is considered by the education, higher education, local government, or some other committee of the legislature, or one of the subcommittees. The New York State legislature was the first to establish in both houses subcommittees dealing exclusively with library matters.

Legislatures make laws and have tried to oversee the operations of the administrative branch, including the state library agency, through the control of administrative rules and regulations.[14] Ideas for library legislation come mainly from professional library interest groups, although some proposals, particularly those that propose amendments in existing laws to deal with problems that the agency has run into, will come from the state library agency. The major characteristic of such changes in library legislation is the provision of broader authority to the state library agency "to promote, develop, and supervise library service for the entire state."[15] Legislators, however, draw their knowledge mainly from within the legislature itself. Factors such as their party and party leaders, as well as legislative specialists, committees, and staff, influence the decisions legislators make on policies. There are always a few legislators who have the knowledge and the interest in the area of public librarianship and who might also have the regard of their colleagues in the legislature. Legislatures, however, are also influenced by interest groups and by their constituents, as well as by the governor and executive agencies. The fact that there are public libraries and public librarians in almost all legislative districts is also an important factor.

The legislative role in public library policy making has not changed greatly. Public library service remains of limited interest to legislators. Still, legislatures have the ultimate responsibility in state library financing and for appropriating state aid to public libraries. While legislators' sentiment toward the public library is generally favorable, and while public library services are highly regarded by them, legislators seldom consider public library service a major or an important issue.

Governors

As a state's chief executive, the governor has control over the decision-making process in the state and can define state issues. The governor is also responsible for managing state government. The visibility of the governor and the available resources enable him or her to select and emphasize those policy issues deemed important. Considerable variations exist among the states as to the powers of the governor. Public librarianship has seldom been an issue of concern to governors; they have seldom given emphasis to library issues or become involved in library policy making. The significance of the governor to library policy has traditionally been minimal. In their state-of-the-state, inaugural, or budget messages, governors rarely mention library issues.[16] Leadership by the governor in public librarianship is most often nonexistent, because governors tend to limit the exercise of their administrative roles to those departments that come within the purview of their appointment power. When it does exist it appears sporadically, reflecting the character and interests of particular governors. The governor's support of a legislative item dealing with public librarianship may help this legislation; a veto may destroy or at least postpone it.

In formulating policy proposals, governors tend to draw

mainly upon their own staff advisers for advice. State librarians are generally of minor importance to the governor as a source of advice on public librarianship. There may be a member of the governor's staff whose responsibilities include public librarianship, but the governor's office fails to provide regular policy leadership for the development of public library policy in the state. Some do so, of course, but generally episodically and only on limited issues. The most significant factor in the governor's influence on public librarianship is the executive budgetary power and the governor's crucial involvement in financial decisions.

Governors do not dominate the administrative machinery of their states, and some of them may not even seek to influence administrative activities. "Governors are not the chief administrators of state government—not because they lack formal powers over administration, but because they are apparently personally incapable or disinclined to use those powers which they possess. Governors appear to be more inclined to be managers rather than policy leaders."[17]

State Library Agencies

The implementation stage in state library policy involves the state library agency. The role of state library bureaucrats, however, extends beyond carrying out state library policies. State library agencies' officials have broad discretionary authority in implementing public library policy. They are also expected to know more than anyone else in state government about public library problems and programs. That the state library agency can play only a peripheral role in state government is due to the fact that only 0.07 percent of states' expenditures are spent for state library agencies, and the budgets of most state library agencies are small.[18]

There is much variety among state library agencies. This variety is due to the historical development of the agency, state law and the legal status of the agency, its position in the state governmental structure, geographic and economic factors, the political subculture of the state, and the political style of elected state officials.

In 1983 twenty-one state library agencies were independent agencies, seventeen were located in the department of Education, three were under the secretary of state, five in other departments of the executive branch, three were reporting directly to the governor, and two were located in the legislative branch.[19] A major trend in state library agencies has been a reduction in the number of independent agencies and an increase in the number of agencies that are a part of the executive branch. The department of education is still the most common executive department in which the state library agency is placed, but agencies may be located in the department of community affairs, the department of community and economic development, the department of cultural resources, the department of culture, recreation and tourism, or the department of higher education.

Changes in the location of the state library agency within state government have been frequent in the last two decades. Many of them resulted in the integration of the state library agency into the state's overall executive organization. Although it is often assumed that the state library agency's place in state government is an important factor in the agency's ability to command resources and political strength,[20] the state library agency's place in state government has little political significance. St. Angelo and associates concluded that strong state library programs are the result of state library leadership and can exist in any state political environment. "Library programs are not limited or encouraged by the level of a state's economy, social development, educational programs, political conditions, or administrative structure.... Agencies in any administrative structure are capable of developing strong programs."[21]

Many members of the library bureaucracy are still "locals," librarians who were born, educated, recruited, and served in small towns and rural areas in their own states. These qualities generate a certain parochialism in defining public library service and proper state-local relations. One of the results of this situation is that state library agencies are often of little value to metropolitan libraries.[22]

A study conducted in the early 1970s reported that many state library agencies were understaffed and underfinanced and "have insufficient influence and visibility to gain the resources and strength they need. Generally, they do not have equal status with other state agencies."[23] Jean Wellisch and associates found that the role of the state library agency in lobbying for state funds "could be best described as active, affirmative, but of low visibility."[24]

Much of the expansion in state library agencies during the 1960s and 1970s came from federal aid. The federal library legislation contained a "single-agency" requirement, which designated the state library agency as the state agency formally responsible to carry out the federal library grant program. Furthermore, the state library agency was given much discretion to set its own priorities and preferences. The Library Services and Construction Act built an "elaborate state agency bureaucracy."[25] It added immensely to the power of state agencies both in their states and in the library profession's legislative programs. The state library agencies not only obtained funds that would not have been available to them otherwise, but they also formed an alliance with the federal library agency. This alliance

formed and perfected through the working of the grant system, can become a powerful force in state politics, perhaps the dominant force in the making of policy for the program in question. When federal and state agencies work together, each reinforces the influence of the other, the state agency gaining as a result of the federal partnership.[26]

Daniel Elazar suggests: "Though the conditions attached by Congress and the federal administrative agencies in the name of Congress are unquestionably important ones, federal control is practically lessened by the powers of state government utilized by state agencies to preserve areas of discretion within which they remain free to act relatively unencumbered by outside rules and regulations."[27] There has been limited gubernatorial supervision of state library administration as well as little legislative oversight.

State Library Boards

The majority of state library boards or commissions are appointed by the governor, although some board members must have certain qualifications to be appointed. Some boards are composed of ex-officio members in all or in part. State board members, as members of a lay governing board, serve on a part-time basis, lack expertise and have limited state resources. The majority of people appointed to the state library board were previously unfamiliar with its activities.

The scope and strength of the policy-making influence of a state board depend largely on the power, interest, and skill of the other participants in the state library policy system. The policy-making resources accessible to a state board, along with the willingness of its members to apply these resources are factors that affect state board influence. The policy-making resources of the state library board are not many; the board has legal authority but little beyond that. Much of their time in board service is spent on functions other than policy making. "Although state boards have clear legal powers and are active in a variety of ways, they are basically impotent."[28]

State library boards tend to be minor participants in establishing state library policy. They have little capability as participants in the library policy arena, and their policy-making role in the legislative arena is marginal. The board members are so dependent on and so overshadowed by the state librarian in the library agency as to raise doubts about what policy-making functions, if any, they perform beyond those legally required.

State library board members do not represent the public effectively. They do not represent all segments of the public, but are composed of only a narrow range of people. Indeed, state library board members are similar to local public library board members in composition.

The board generally appoints the state librarian, but has no control in practice over that bureaucrat. The state librarian prepares the agenda, provides the staff for the board, and is the source of almost all ideas and information received by the board. As a result, state library boards do not oversee the state librarian effectively.

The two perceived weaknesses of state boards are the traditional apolitical posture of the board and its lack of visibility to the legislature and to many legislators. Library board members have no clear channels through which they may exercise their legal authority. Their legal powers do not provide them with financial independence or direct access to monetary resources. The legislature and the governor have the authority to decide on the amount of money to be spent for public librarianship and the purposes for which the money should be spent. The legislature enacts the laws determining the state's basic fiscal policy. To obtain the resources for the state library agency as well as for the public libraries in the state, board members must have the capacity to influence state legislators. State boards do not have a tradition of political involvement nor are they able to mobilize constituents of importance to politicians. Few board members have any political experience nor do they develop political contacts or interests. They view their role as being above politics and prefer to have little to do with legislation or politics. They do not see the possibility of trying to influence the legislature and seeking the introduction of legislation because their influence is very low. State boards seldom take a lead in promoting library legislation. Although the governor's office may be a crucial access point, the board has little working relationship with the governor or his staff and has been a very minor source of ideas and advice for the governor's office. Board members are not included in the inner council of gubernatorial advisers.

State library board members are ineffective leaders. With a few exceptions, such as the state educational boards in New York and Texas (public libraries are only a very small part of their concern), there is little evidence that most state boards seek to exert influence on legislatures or on the budgetary process by trying to mobilize supporters or arousing the public.

State Librarians

The chief officers of the state library agency are commonly called state librarians. They are all appointed officials, generally appointed by the state library board or by the official in charge of the department in which the state library agency is located. Only a few state librarians (for example, in California) are appointed by the governor and serve "at his pleasure." While some state librarians consider themselves managers and not policy makers, the majority are deeply involved in setting the state library agency's policy as well as implementing it. State librarians have control over both the issues that appear before the state library board and the information about these issues supplied to members of the board. State librarians establish the agenda of the board meetings, and the approval of the chairman of the board is pro forma. State librarians follow the "rule of anticipated reactions" in anticipating what board members want or need in preparing the agenda. State library board members expect the state librarian to exert a leadership role on policy issues. It is the state librarian who advances policy proposals to which the board reacts. Only seldom do policy proposals advanced by the state librarian encounter overt resistance, and only seldom do board members manifest opposition to such policy proposals. Although arguments may occur between board members and the state librarians, they are seldom shared with the public. State librarians formulate their policy proposals in detail and bring them to their boards for legitimation most of the time. The board seldom gives the state librarian real direction but only formalizes the state librarian's policy recommendations.

State librarians exert great influence in the state library agency arena but have little influence in the legislative arena, since they are all appointed officials. State librarians appointed by the governor cannot always lobby in the legislature against the governor. This may also be the case for state librarians appointed by other executive officers and even those appointed by the legislature. Most state library agencies and state librarians who try to lobby the legislature have to work behind the scenes. A recent guide stated, "Do not count on the state library to initiate a legislative program, or actively spearhead a lobbying effort."[29] They are, however, the source of much of the legislation that affects the state library agency itself.

STATE LIBRARY INTEREST GROUPS

The two major library interest groups on the state level concerned with public librarianship are the state library association and the state library trustee association. These two associations often work in concert and have even combined to hire a lobbyist. The state library association continues to play the leadership role in obtaining library legislation and in convincing legislators to sponsor and introduce library bills. In several states, separate statewide organizations of lay library supporters, such as state Friends of the Library or citizens' councils have also been established. The direction of legislative activity and the policies and priorities that the state library association pursues are usually determined by its governing body. Several state library associations have been employing and using professional staff and a paid lobbyist to lobby the legislature.

State library associations often work in cooperation with the state library agency. Since the library association is both a professional association and an interest group, there is a strong feeling of loyalty between the association and the state library agency. The state library association and the library agency often cooperate to produce standards for public libraries. Such standards may be used by the library association and by public libraries as an instrument for requesting additional funding. Indeed, in small states, the library association depends on the state library agency a great deal.

The basic resources of interest groups are the number of their members, the status of their members, and money. In terms of sheer number of members and the amount of money available to them (which comes mainly from dues), library interest groups have little power. Only six state library associations have more than 2,000 members; thirty-two associations have fewer than 1,000; and ten associations have fewer than 500 members.[30] State library associations cannot deliver votes. Considering their small size, however, state library associations have been quite effective.

As a result of the state preconferences preceding the 1979 White House Conference on Library and Information Services, statewide lay support groups have been established in many states. Most of these groups are concerned with public relations activities; few act as lobbies. Political action committees (PACs) have been established in a few states, such as Virginia. Library groups, however, have few financial resources for political campaigns. Their major power, that is, their capacity to affect policy enactment and provide information, comes from staff contacts and local members' contacts with legislators and legislative leaders, since legislative influence is most effectively applied where legislators live.

Although the majority of librarians are substantially less interested in politics than those who lobby in their name, one of the most important tools used by library interest groups on the state level has been statewide legislative networks. Another tool has been the creation of library coalitions between various library groups and between these groups and nonlibrary groups. Preventing the fragmentation of the public library lobby has been particularly important. State library associations and other groups lobbying the legislature have succeeded in building consensus and reducing the areas of disagreement in public librarianship. They try to speak with one voice and to agree on a legislative program. Still, library interests may split and there may be disagreements between the state library agency and the library association, which can cause a fragmentation of effort leading to the immobilization of the library lobby.

STATE MANDATES

Mandates are responsibilities, procedures, and activities that are imposed by the state on public libraries or on local governments in ways that affect public libraries, by legislative, administrative, or judicial action.[31] Mandates place limits or additional requirements on public libraries. They constrain the public library's boundaries of choice and substitute state for local priorities. Furthermore, while the state might mandate certain actions, the money with which to carry out these actions is not always provided, and the state lets local officials figure how to pay for them.

Mandates are often used to achieve statewide uniformity of service levels for public libraries, to require library services meeting minimum state standards, to prescribe more professional standards for librarians, and other statewide objectives.

A mandate is imposed as a direct order or as a condition of aid. Mandates may state what a public library should do, how it should be done, and how resources are to be spent. State mandates relate to the organization and procedures of the public library, the holding of local elections, or the designation of library board members and their responsibilities. Mandates may dictate the quality or the quantity of the services to be provided by the public library, such as library hours. Many states also have reporting mandates. State mandates may put a cap on the public library's expenditures or on the library tax rate. States may mandate public libraries' participation in library systems as a condition of receiving state aid. Indeed, states use state aid to require public libraries to meet mandatory minimum standards of public library service or to levy a minimum rate of library tax, to prevent local communities from reducing the expenditures from their own resources for the public library. While state mandates have not substantially altered the activities of the public libraries, they have added to the cost of their operations. There is, however, no systematic state inspection system of public libraries. State enforcement of many mandates has been sporadic, and public library accountability is seldom investigated at state level.

The increase in state mandates contradicts the most powerful claim for the local public library—that the citizens are endowed with independence and freedom in making their own decisions about their public library. Discretion of local public administrators contracts as the state minimum specifications expand and the number of rules and regulations affecting the public library grow. The states assume greater control of the public library with the help of state aid to public libraries, which provides the state with a direct tool to enforce its mandates.

STATE PUBLIC LIBRARY FINANCE

State aid has grown enormously over the past two decades because state spending in general has increased. States provide more financial resources for their local governments, although much of state assistance results not from a sense of altruism but from pressure by local governments and interest groups. State aid to public libraries is a relatively new responsibility for most state governments. The majority of states have enacted some state aid legislation, but states make different efforts in financing public librarianship. In fiscal year 1982, states were the source of 7.7 percent of public library funding. In fiscal year 1984, thirteen states had no direct state aid to public libraries at all, and six states had no state aid whatsoever. But fifteen states had more than $1.00 per capita state aid to public libraries (Table 14).

The growth and diversification of states' revenue sources in the last twenty years provided many states with the capacity to make available increased funding for public libraries and thus increase the states' role in public librarianship. While there is no necessary connection between state control and state aid, the dependence on state funds by local public libraries has increased the shift of primary political arena of public librarianship from the local level to the state level.

There are inequities in state library finance because state aid to public libraries is based primarily on per capita formula; funds are allocated in proportion to population. Few states provide equalization grants, state aid distributed in relation to local fiscal capacity or local fiscal effort. Only nine states have some equalization formula to allocate grants to public libraries. It is not politically possible to provide state aid that is not based on a per capita or a flat rate formula because of the opposition from suburban communities. Equity of financial resources has not become yet a fundamental issue involving the raising and allocating of state revenue for the public libraries, perhaps because state library boards and state library agencies have been marginal participants in state library financial policy.

Some states have used state aid to encourage reorganization of public libraries and to force public libraries to join library systems. Still, some municipalities have been willing to forgo state aid in order to retain control over their public libraries.[32]

Table 14
Per Capita State Aid to Public Libraries, by State, 1984

State	Direct Aid to Public Libraries	Total State Aid to Public Libraries
Alabama	0.49	0.49
Alaska	1.35	1.96
Arizona	0.10	0.10
Arkansas	0.92	0.92
California	0.74	0.84
Colorado	0.17	0.52
Connecticut	0.32	0.74
Delaware	0.44	0.44
Florida	0.53	0.59
Georgia	1.95	1.95
Idaho	0	0
Illinois	0.48	1.91
Indiana	0.17	0.32
Iowa	0	0.38
Kansas	0.17	0,32
Kentucky	0.28	0.75
Louisiana	0.25	0.25
Maine	0.11	0.30
Maryland	2.38	3.25
Massachusetts	0.76	1.77
Michigan	1.39	1.70
Minnesota	0	1.16
Mississippi	0.66	0.66
Missouri	0.32	0.32
Montana	0	0.61
Nebraska	0.11	0.36
Nevada	0.16	0.16
New Hampshire	0	0
New Jersey	1.07	1.43
New Mexico	0.17	0.17
New York	1.53	2.96
North Carolina	0.79	0.79
North Dakota	0.81	0.81
Ohio	0.01	0.10
Oklahoma	0.41	0.45
Oregon	0.08	0.08
Pennsylvania	1.35*	1.35
Rhode Island	0.47	2.25
South Dakota	0	0
Tennessee	0	1.40
Texas	0	0.30
Utah	0	0
Vermont	0	0.73
Virginia	1.76	1.76
Washington	0	0
West Virginia	2.86*	2.87
Wisconsin	0	1.28
Wyoming	0	0

*Aid to public and multitype library systems and networks
included.

Source: The ALA Yearbook of Library and Information Services
'85, p. 289; U.S. Bureau of the Census, Statistical
Abstract of the United States 1985 (Washington, D.C.:
GPO, 1985), p. 11.

CONCLUSION

State role in public librarianship has grown in importance and state control of public libraries, using a variety of mechanisms, particularly state aid to public libraries, has been increasing.

NOTES

1. Daniel J. Elazar, "The New Federalism: Can the States Be Trusted?" *The Public Interest*, no. 35 (Spring 1974): 90.

2. Jerome T. Murphy, "Progress and Problems: The Paradox of State Reform," in *Policymaking in Education*, ed. Ann Lieberman and Milbrey W. McLaughlin (Chicago: University of Chicago Press, 1982), p. 203.

3. Advisory Commission on Intergovernmental Relations, *State and Local Roles in the Federal System* (Washington, D.C.: GPO, 1982), pp. 16–17, 20–21.

4. John Kincaid, "Political Quality of Urban Life," in *Political Culture, Public Policy and the American States*, ed. John Kincaid (Philadelphia: Institute for the Study of Human Issues, 1982), p. 123.

5. Daniel J. Elazar, *American Federalism: A View from the States*, 3d ed. (New York: Harper & Row, 1984), pp. 114–122.

6. Douglas St. Angelo et al., *State Library Policy, Its Legislative and Environmental Context* (Chicago: ALA, 1971), p. 3.

7. Advisory Commission on Intergovernmental Relations, *State and Local Role in the Federal System*, p. 62.

8. Kenneth E. Beasley, "The Changing Role of the State Library," *Advances in Librarianship* 2 (1971): 197.

9. Laurence Iannaccone, *Politics in Education* (New York: The Center for Applied Research in Education, 1967), pp. 42–50.

10. Roald F. Campbell and Tim L. Mazzoni, Jr., eds., *State Policy Making for the Public Schools* (Berkeley, Calif.: McCutchan, 1976).

11. Government Studies and Systems, Inc., *The Role of the State in the Development of Public Library Services* (Washington, D.C.: U.S. Office of Education, 1974), pp. 15–16.

12. U.S. Bureau of the Census, *State Government Finances in 1982* (Washington, D.C.: GPO, 1983), Table 9.

13. St. Angelo et al., *State Library Policy*, p. 37.

14. Alan Rosenthal, "Legislative Oversight and the Balance of Power in State Government," *State Government* 56 (1983): 90–98.

15. Beasley, "The Changing Role of the State Library," pp. 187–213.

16. Eric B. Herzik, "Governors and Issues: A Typology of Concerns," *State Government* 56 (1983): 58–64.

17. Gleen Abney and Thomas P. Lauth, "The Governor as Chief Administrator," *Public Administration Review* 43 (January/February 1983): 48.

18. U.S. Bureau of the Census, *State Government Finances: 1981* (Washington, D.C.: GPO, 1982), Table 9; *The Book of the States 1982–83*, p. 305.

19. *The State Library Agencies: A Survey Project Report 1983*, 6th ed. (Chicago: ASCLA, 1983).

20. F. William Sommers, "The State Library Agencies: An Overview," in *The State Library Agencies: A Survey Project Report, 1983*, 6th ed. (Chicago, ASCLA, 1983), p. 2.

21. St. Angelo, *State Library Policy*, p. 63.

22. Ibid.; Ralph Blasingame, "The Potential Leadership Role of the State Library," in *State-wide Library Planning: The New Jersey Example*, ed. Mary Virginia Gaver (New Brunswick, N.J.: Rutgers University Press, 1969), pp. 97–110.

23. Jean Wellisch et al., *The Public Library and Federal Policy* (Westport, Conn.: Greenwood Press, 1974), p. 36.

24. Ibid., p. 33.

25. John Berry, "Amend LSCA Now," *Library Journal* 100 (March 1, 1975), p. 425.

26. Martha Derthick, *The Influence of Federal Grants: Public Assistance in Massachusetts* (Cambridge, Mass.: Harvard University Press, 1970), p. 206.

27. Elazar, *American Federalism*, p. 181.

28. Gerald E. Stroufe, "State School Board Members and Educational Policy," *Administrator's Notebook* 19 (October 1970): 1–4.

29. Dean Burgess, Patricia Grosbeck, and Diana Young, *Getting It Passed* (Chicago: Library Administration and Management Association, 1984), p. 13.

30. American Library Association, Chapter Relations Officer, "Membership Statistics of State and Regional Library Associations," June 1983.

31. Advisory Commission on Intergovernmental Relations, *State Mandating of Local Expenditures* (Washington, D.C.: GPO, 1978); Catherine H. Lovell et al., *Federal and State Mandating on Local Governments: An Exploration of Issues and Impacts* (Riverside, Calif.: University of California, 1979).

32. Malcolm Getz, *Public Libraries: An Economic View* (Baltimore: Johns Hopkins University Press, 1980), p. 158.

8

The Politics of Public Librarianship at the Federal Level

The growth of the federal government in almost all areas has been phenomenal. It is reflected in the multiplicity of functions in which the federal government is involved, the extensive penetration of its influence into state and local administrations, and the growing financial dependence of state and local governments on federal funds.

NATIONAL PUBLIC LIBRARY POLICY

Public librarianship is not a political issue on the national level. For example, the desegregation of public libraries has never been the national issue that the desegregation of schools has been. A coherent, widely shared, and clearly stated and understood national policy on public librarianship, supporting and strengthening public libraries in the United States, has never been set forth. John Frantz stated the point well:

One reason for the recently recognized vulnerability of federal library grant programs is probably that the authorizing legislation came into being not by presenting a coherent, organized rationale for library assistance, but rather by shrewd and skillful exploitation of political opportunities.... The Library Services Act of 1956 ... was the first in a series of essentially *ad hoc* components of a federal library policy.... Despite the flowering of library assistance programs, the garden had never been systematically planned, graded, or even landscaped.... There was not then, and there is not now, rational articulation of the functions of libraries in the achievement of national goals.[1]

The federal library policy has been described as "confused" and "fuzzy."[2] While the Library Services and Construction Act (LSCA) is the most important piece of federal public library legislation, that legislation "projects neither the concept nor the urging of a Federal role in developing and maintaining a program of public library services designed to meet the informational, educational, and cultural needs of an industrialized nation."[3] The National Advisory Commission on Libraries recommended

that it be declared National Policy, enunciated by the President and enacted into law by the Congress, that the American people should be provided with library and informational services adequate to their needs, and that the Federal Government, in collaboration with state and local governments and private agencies, should exercise leadership in assuring the provision of such services.[4]

The most coherent declaration of a national public library policy and purpose appeared in a legislative bill that was never enacted. The National Library Act introduced in 1979 stated that the policy of the United States would be "to promote universal library and information services, provide all persons access to information on public programs ... and free, equal and open access to all publicly funded library and information services." The purpose of the National Library Act would have been "to promote and assist inter-library cooperation; public library services, construction, and special programs," and at the same time "to preserve the tradition of local control."[5]

The idea behind the National Library Act, to insure a minimum standard of public library service to all citizens throughout the United States, was significant only because it marked a shift from the view that public libraries are primarily a local responsibility. The fact that the National Library Act never even reached the congressional committee stage is perhaps one indication of the problems involved with a function considered by many, among them librarians, to be one in which the federal government should not be involved.

Still, the federal government is involved in public librarianship to some extent, and in fiscal year 1982, it provided 3.7 percent of the funding for public librarianship.[6]

Although the federal government has become involved with public library policy making, it has assumed no responsibility for the direct operation of public libraries, and so far it has not acquired significant power regarding public librarianship. Because of the objections of state governments, no direct federal-local relations in the area of public librarianship have been developed. Cessation of all federal funds will not bring the closing of public libraries throughout the nation and probably will not even curtail library service, although it will have an impact on many state library agencies and their services.

Of the many participants involved in public librarianship in the federal arena, only two groups play major roles. These groups are the members and the staff aides of the education subcommittees of Congress who specialize in public library issues, and the library interest group. These groups have pushed for a national involvement in public librarianship. Other participants, such as the president, the staff of the Office of Management and Budget, the members of congressional appropriations and budget committees, the federal bureaucracy (and particularly the staff of the Department of Education), the courts, the political parties, and the press play only minor roles or no role at all, nor do some of them wish to play any other role.[7]

Not even mentioned in the U.S. Constitution, public librarianship is a function that is considered to be a state (and a local) responsibility rather than a federal one. Placing public librarianship on the national agenda and involving the federal government in it through the provision of federal aid to public libraries, albeit indirectly, is justified by federal officials under the constitutional power of the federal government to advance the general welfare, and to ameliorate national social needs through the improvement of conditions in various parts of the nation.

Congress

Policy making in Congress is decentralized and fragmented. Congressional policy making is dominated by committees and is committee centered. Membership on a committee gives members expertise, a voice in policy formulation, and bargaining leverage with their peers and the executive branch.[8] Indeed, the subcommittees have the power; they are independent power centers and function with considerable autonomy. "The structure, procedure, and culture of Congress tend to obscure the general interest, encourage particularism, and create an environment in which organized interest groups and special pleaders can be assured a sympathetic response."[9]

Once a matter is identified as an issue, specific remedies must be formulated, further information gathered, and the relevant interests sought out and accommodated. Sufficient political force must be mobilized to hammer out a definitive legislative compromise and secure its enactment.

Congressmen have three basic goals: reelection, influence within the House, and good public policy. Members seek not only electoral security but also power, prestige, and preferment within Congress and the government establishment. Members of the Education and Labor Committee, the committee responsible for public librarianship in the House of Representatives, emphasize a strong personal interest in, and a concern for, the content of public policy in their committee's subject matter.

Four clusters of "outsiders" are likely to have an interest in committee behavior with the capacity to influence such behavior: (1) members of the parent chamber, (2) the executive branch, (3) interest groups, and (4) the political parties.[10] These outside, and sometimes contending clusters, seek to influence the members of the education committees. Members must contend with all these influences and pursue their goals in a pluralistic environment. The Labor and Education committees are probably the most ideological and partisan committees in Congress and, as such, are subjected to considerable pressure.

Education and Labor members come to their Committee to make good public policy. They inhabit a distinctly pluralistic and partisan environment and they happily operate as integral elements of the party-led policy coalitions in that environment. Their key decision rules prescribe a blend of policy partisanship and policy individualism. And their internal decision-making processes bear the imprint of those two rules.[11]

The power within the committee is earned by specialization. To make a name for oneself in Congress, a member must be a specialist. John Fogarty, chairman of the House Appropriations Subcommittee considering the budget of the Department of Health, Education and Welfare, became a library specialist because "there was no one else in the House, in the 1950's, who could be called a library champion," and because he realized that he was not going to compete with others' pet causes.[12]

Each policy has two critical dimensions: the degree of conflict it entails, and the public salience (that is, the conspicuousness) that members of Congress perceive it to possess. The level of conflict regarding public librarianship is low, and the public salience is medium or low. Members of Congress wishing to gain visibility and a reputation for policy leadership find issues in the high-salience, low-conflict area attractive;[13] public librarianship is not such an issue. Because library policy does not have a broad impact on society (and in that sense, is not greatly important) it also has a weak, if any, partisan content.

The initiative for library legislation has always come from Congress rather than from the president or the executive branch. All library legislation that has emerged from Congress has been shaped by a small group of legislators who exercise power in the subcommittees having jurisdiction over public librarianship, the Subcommittee on Postsecondary Education of the Committee on Education and Labor of the House of Representatives and the Subcommittee on Education, Arts and Humanities of the Committee on Labor and Human Resources of the Senate. "One finding stands out as tall as the Washington

Monument: Of all the actors contributing to rapid growth in federal functions...it is the individual, hyper-responsive congressional entrepreneur who is most often responsible."[14] It is no wonder that the administrations' proposals to reduce or eliminate federal funding for public librarianship tend to confront congressional resistance, particularly from those congressmen who consider that program as "their own."

"Ostensibly, congressional hearings are important primarily as fact-finding instruments.... Much of the information, however, is available to committee members long before the hearings take place.... The positions of the administration and the special interest groups are well known, and, in all likelihood, executive branch officials and pressure group lobbyists have already presented their views to committee members well in advance of the hearings."[15] Officials of the federal library agency reiterate the policy of the president and the Office of Management and Budget, with which they may not agree. The fact that the Education Subcommittee's position on library legislation has often been decided before the hearings can be clearly perceived by following these hearings. Almost all witnesses are pro-legislation, and witnesses who disagree with the bill are treated unfavorably by the subcommittee's chair.[16] Congress, however, does not generally follow through on its legislation to see whether it was carried out properly and effectively, perhaps because it is not sure what it really wanted the program to achieve.

The President

Public librarianship has never been a policy issue in presidential politics and has rarely received presidential attention. Presidents see no advantage in active support for federal aid to public libraries. Presidents may make public statements about the importance of public libraries, but nothing else. "All library legislation...has remained outside the mainstream of presidential and executive-branch endorsements."[17]

Whether it is the appointment of the librarian of Congress, or the members of the National Commission on Libraries and Information Service, the library interest group had little success with the president. This is due partly to ALA's political naïveté and to the fact that too few librarians are actively involved in politics.

The president's power over the budget as well as the budget and appropriations process in Congress have led to a series of president-versus-Congress clashes over the amount of money available for libraries. The president and Congress have done battle several times on library legislation, particularly over the reauthorization of the LSCA and the appropriations for it. The executive branch has tried several times to terminate the categorical library program, based on the proposition that the program already achieved its goals, through "the program's past success at establishing the highest practical levels of access across the country to library service" and the assertion that public library services should be a state and local responsibility.[18] As Republican administrations have found when they opposed the expansion of the public library programs or when they tried to eliminate them, it is politically difficult to kill a program if it has staunch supporters in Congress and an active lobby.

The Courts

There has been little influence by federal judicial decisions on public librarianship matters. The only exceptions may have been decisions on issues of intellectual freedom and on freedom of information, which have only an indirect impact on public libraries. The recent court decision legitimizing the professional library degree may have implications for public library staffing.

Advisory Commissions

As far as local public libraries are concerned, advisory commissions have had no significant impact. The National Advisory Commission on Libraries (NACL) confirms this point.[19] The constituency for the NACL was not the public libraries or even the ALA. The initiative for the establishment of the commission was a concern over the role of the Library of Congress and research libraries, and the immediate initiator of the commission was the Committee on Scientific and Technical Information (COSATI). Recommendations received from academic librarians led several assistants to President Lyndon Johnson to propose, over a period of four years, a presidential commission. The Bureau of the Budget was not enthusiastic about the commission because of the danger that it might simply become a lobby for increasing federal aid to libraries. That same fear was also present in the Department of Health, Education and Welfare. When the advisory commission was created, none of the original members represented public library interest. Outside criticisms led to the appointment of one public librarian as a member of the commission. (Two other members were lay leaders were appointed because of pressure from powerful members of Congress.) President Johnson never showed any personal interest in the commission. Indeed, he was never "sensitive" to the library cause. His only concern about the advisory commission was that there would be "some good Texans on it." The only concrete result of the NACL recommendations has been the establishment of the National Commission on Libraries and Information Science (NCLIS).

Interest groups, such as the American Library Association (ALA), seek the creation of a new federal agency to enhance its status in the outside community. "For many, organization is a symbol." Organizations such as the National Commission on Libraries and Information Science "are more important as evidence of national concern than as molders of federal policies."[20] Based upon a recommendation from the National Advisory Commission on Libraries, the ALA sponsored the legislation to create the NCLIS. In spite of the objection of the Nixon administration, the commission was created by Congress in 1970. In light of the president's opposition (although President Nixon signed the bill creating the commission, he did so grudgingly), "the libraries' victory in achieving their first permanent presidential advisory commission might best be described as pyrrhic."[21] Presidents have not supported the commission since its creation.

The president appoints the commissioners of the NCLIS, but the commission is supposed to be independent of the control, direction, and interference from the president. The ALA, which lobbied hard for the creation of the commission, "has had a consistently dismal record in gaining representation on the Commission."[22]

The White House Conference on Library and Information Services

The most important purpose of the White House Conference on Library and Information Services was the provision of visibility to the library profession. "Such convocations are the focus of much publicity—but celebration rather than cerebration usually predominates."[23] Since the national government has been setting national goals in most domestic areas, the library profession also wanted to obtain the federal government legitimation through the White House Conference. Similarly, the resolution introduced in the House of Representatives calling for a new White House conference states that the purpose of this conference is "to build public awareness of the precarious state of American library service and to facilitate informed, grassroots policymaking concerning the future of all types of libraries."[24]

FEDERAL LIBRARY AGENCY

The Department of Education (and its predecessor, the Office of Education) has little to do with library policy making, although the secretary of education (and his predecessor, the commissioner of education) has the formal responsibility for the implementation of the federal library policy.

The first Library Services Division was established in 1938 in the Office of Education. It changed from a section to a branch, to a division, and (temporarily) to a bureau, and then back to a division, and finally to an office, all within the Office of Education, later the Department of Education. "The library lobby's campaign for bureau status ... indicates a belief that the result would increase the prestige of library aid programs, provide a power base to achieve more of the agency's objec-

tives, and establish direct access to the Commissioner of
Education."[25]

The federal library agency became in 1985 a unit within the
Office of Educational Research and Improvement under an Assistant Secretary in the Department of Education. This reorganization was welcomed, with reservations, by the library
profession. The ALA Washington Office reported in its
newsletter:

the effect of the reorganization on libraries would be to remove a layer
of bureaucracy between the head of the library unit and the Assistant
Secretary, and to remove allied educational technology programs, thus
both elevating and isolating the library unit. The real effect may
depend on the leadership of the library unit.[26]

The Department of Education was created by President
Carter as a reward for the powerful political support of the
National Education Association and other educational interests groups. The library interest groups have not had the resources that the educational interest groups have, but they
have tried to have in the Department of Education their "own"
agency.

Executive agencies are susceptible to domination by their
clientele group and by congressional committees. Between the
congressional committees, the federal agency, and the clientele
group an "iron triangle" is created. "Those who are program
advocates in the beginning become program protectors along
the way. They may criticize here and there, cut back or defer
fund authorizations as circumstances dictate, call for evaluations and reports when trouble spots appear, but they do not
propose to jettison the programs they have authorized, and
continue to authorize over the years."[27]

The administrative agency needs the support of the interest
group. The result is that the supporting interest group is placed,
either openly or tacitly, in the agency decision making process.
"What the federal agency undertakes depends in part on what
its state counterpart desires or can be expected to concur in,
for the state agency's cooperation is essential to the realization
of any federal goal."[28] For example, the Office of Education

went to its clients, the state library agencies, to help write the regulations for the LSA. The state librarians were involved in writing the regulations for the library legislation that they should follow in implementing the law. The federal library agency also provides the library interest group with information needed by that group and by its allies in Congress.

FEDERAL AID

Local public libraries may benefit from several acts of Congress. In 1979 Elazar found at least thirty different federal grants that had the potential to provide funds to libraries.[29] The most important federal legislation as far as public libraries are concerned have been the Library Services Act (LSA), and later, the Library Services and Construction Act (LSCA). Between 1956 and 1982 Congress appropriated over $1.1 billion under these acts. Much of the federal money, however, did not reach the local pubic libraries but was retained at the state level.

Congress has become very fond of the grant-in-aid idea. This enthusiasm . . . reflects pressure from federal agencies, functional specialists in and out of government, and special interest groups, all of whom realize that it is possible to obtain action in all states by applying leverage at one pressure point only—the Congress. So, both interest groups and congressmen are major defenders of the current grant system.[30]

The purpose of federal aid is to stimulate as efficiently as possible the achievement of certain fairly narrow federal objectives and stimulate the states to launch or expand services for which states and local governments are regarded as responsible. "Politically speaking, federal aid programs are an outcome of a loose coalition which resorts to a mixed federal state program because it is not strong enough in individual states to secure its program."[31]

A federal grant-in-aid to public libraries is a closed-end formula categorical grant. It is a specific, narrowly defined grant made for a special purpose. The grant specifies the total amount available and provides that each recipient state will receive a proportional share of the total depending on conformance to a formula.

Congressional findings relative to the LSCA are as follows:

The role of libraries has expanded to include providing programs to meet the needs of special populations, to help establish networks and share resource materials among a wide variety of libraries; the role of libraries as information centers should be expanded to meet the increasing needs of their communities for informational and educational resources; and the scope and purpose of the Library Services and Construction Act (LSCA) should be expanded to include a broader range of programs which may receive funds and to ensure services to populations which might otherwise be without library service.[32]

The LSCA has been intended to be additive and stimulative, increasing state and local government expenditures for public libraries over and above what they would have been in the absence of the federal grant. In some states, however, it became substitutive and was used by state and local governments to reduce spending from their own sources for public libraries. Projects financed from federal funds were often canceled when federal funding was lessened or terminated.

In awarding a grant-in-aid to state government, one of the most fundamental strategies employed by Congress has been to require a clearly designated and formally responsive state agency to carry out the purposes of the grant. The idea behind the "single state agency" to implement the federal program has been to bring some order to state government. The state library agency was designated such a state agency in the LSA and LSCA. In some states the law brought such an agency into existence in order to receive this federal money.

Once approved, the library legislation survived congressional expansion, modification, and reauthorization as well as attempts by the administration to dispose of it. Modification involved changes of purpose, as well as better reporting and evaluation requirements. Library aid is constrained, however, "by its failure to be perceived as a program advancing a clear national objective.... Regardless of repeated efforts, better library service is not viewed generally as important in and of itself."[33]

Federal aid to libraries went to reinforce traditional programs and for the employment of additional personnel. It made state library agencies more dependent on federal funds and on the federal government. The visibility of the state library agencies and state librarians in lobbying efforts for federal funds is high. The Chief Officers of State Library Agencies (COSLA) fought any interpretation (by the General Accounting Office or the inspector general in the Department of Education) that would reduce the level of discretion they possess. Regardless of some disagreements, all library interest groups prefer federal aid with minimum federal involvement. It is no wonder that the Urban Libraries Council, a group composed of large urban public libraries, would lobby for additional federal funding for urban libraries, and for federal per capita general support grants to public libraries, and that COSLA would lobby hard to maintain the LSCA as a "single state agency" grant.

There has not always been complete agreement between the various groups. The Urban Libraries Council, for example, succeeded in adding in 1977 an amendment to Title I of the LSCA providing the possibility of special funding for urban libraries if appropriations exceed $60 million. ALA and COSLA were initially ambivalent about this amendment, although they eventually accepted it.

GENERAL REVENUE SHARING

The idea behind the State and Local Fiscal Assistance Act of 1972 was to share federal revenues with state and local governments with few restrictions. Local governments were permitted to determine the services for which the money should be used. Public libraries were eligible for participation in general revenue sharing. Indeed, public libraries were one of the eight priority items for the use of these funds on the local level. Public librarians were ambivalent about general revenue sharing because they were concerned they would not be able to compete with other local demands for these funds. On average, public libraries received about 1.5 percent of the federal funds made available to local governments. In fiscal years 1981 through 1983, the amount received by public libraries was some $220 million. General revenue sharing "has been of value in supplementing public library finances."[34]

CITIZEN PARTICIPATION

Many of the federal aid programs require citizen participation in their administration. The LSCA, for example, requires the states to establish state advisory councils on libraries, broadly representative of public, school, academic, special, and institutional libraries. The majority of states have established advisory councils, but they have played only a peripheral role in the administering of federal aid.

CONCLUSION

The educational subcommittees of the Congress remain the locus of the public library policy in the federal government. The executive branch has never considered public librarianship as a national issue and has tried to terminate public library legislation.

NOTES

1. John C. Frantz, "The Role of the Federal Government," *Library Trends* 23 (October 1974): 239–240.

2. Ernest R. DeProspo, Jr., "Federal Funds in Governance of Local Library Institutions: A Reappraisal," *Library Trends* 26 (Fall 1977): 200.

3. Government Studies and Systems, Inc., *Alternatives for Financing the Public Library* (Philadelphia: author, 1974), pp. 63–64.

4. Douglas M. Knight and E. Shepley Nourse, eds., *Libraries at Large: Tradition, Innovation, and the National Interest* (New York: Bowker, 1969), p. 504.

5. *Congressional Record* 126 (June 20, 1980): S7642-S7649.

6. "An NCLIS Library Statistical Sampler," *Library Journal* 110 (October 15, 1985): 35–36.

7. Advisory Commission on Intergovernmental Relations, *An*

Agenda for American Federalism: Restoring Confidence and Competence (Washington, D.C.: GPO, 1981), p. 105.

8. Richard F. Fenno, Jr., *Congressmen in Committees* (Boston: Little, Brown, 1973), p. 15.

9. Harold Seidman, *Politics, Position, and Power: The Dynamics of Federal Organization*, 3d ed. (New York: Oxford University Press, 1980), p. 41.

10. David E. Price, "Congressional Committees in the Policy Process," in *Congress Reconsidered*, 3d ed., ed. Laurence C. Dodd and Bruce L. Oppenheimer (Washington, D.C.: CQ Press, 1985), p. 167.

11. Fenno, *Congressmen in Committees*, p. 226.

12. James S. Healy, *John F. Fogarty: Political Leadership for Library Development* (Metuchen, N.J.: Scarecrow Press, 1974), p. 92.

13. Price, "Congressional Committees in the Policy Process," pp. 183–184.

14. Wayne F. Anderson, "Intergovernmental Aid: Relief or Intrusion?" *National Civic Review* 69 (March 1980): 129.

15. Walter J. Oleszek, *Congressional Procedures and the Policy Process*, 2d ed. (Washington, D.C.: CQ Press, 1984), p. 86.

16. Cf. U.S. House of Representatives, Committee on Education and Labor, Subcommittee on Postsecondary Education, *Oversight Hearings on the Reauthorization of the Library Services and Construction Act*, March 17, 1983. 98th Cong., 1st sess. 1984, p. 115.

17. R. Kathleen Molz, *Federal Policy and Library Support* (Cambridge, Mass.: The MIT Press, 1976), p. 16.

18. Department of Education, "The Fiscal 1985 Budget," February 1, 1984.

19. David Shavit, "President Lyndon Johnson and the National Advisory Commission on Libraries," unpublished paper, 1984.

20. Seidman, *Politics, Position, and Power*, p. 28.

21. R. Kathleen Molz, *National Planning for Library Service, 1935–1975* (Chicago: ALA, 1984), p. 113.

22. Eric Moon, "Our Commission, Our Omission," *Library Journal* 109 (July 1984): 1283–1287.

23. Thomas E. Cronin, "The Presidency and Education," *Phi Delta Kappan* 49 (February 1968): 295.

24. Congressman William Ford, *Congressional Record* 131 (June 19, 1985): H4526g.

25. Advisory Commission on Intergovernmental Relations, *The Federal Role in the Federal System: The Dynamics of Growth: Federal Involvement in Libraries* (Washington, D.C.: GPO 1980), pp. 30–31.

26. *ALA Washington Newsletter* 37 (July 23, 1985): 4.

27. Herbert Roback, "Program Evaluation by and for the Congress," *The Bureaucrat* 5 (April 1976): 27.

28. Martha Derthick, *The Influence of Federal Grants: Public Assistance in Massachusetts* (Cambridge, Mass.: Harvard University Press, 1970), p. 207.

29. Daniel J. Elazar, *American Federalism: A View from the States*, 3d ed. (New York: Harper & Row, 1984), p. 87.

30. Anita S. Herbert, *Federal Grants-in-Aid: Maximizing Benefits to the States* (New York: Praeger, 1976), p. 12.

31. Phillip Monypenny, "Federal Grants-in-Aid to State Governments: A Political Analysis," *National Tax Journal* 13 (March 1960): 15.

32. U.S. Congress, Senate, Committee on Labor and Human Resources, *Library Services and Construction Act Amendments of 1984.* 98th Cong., 2d sess., 1984 (Senate Report 98–486), p. 12.

33. Advisory Commission on Intergovernmental Relations, *Federal Involvement in Libraries*, p. 38.

34. Frank Goudy, "A Piece of the Pie: Libraries and General Revenue Sharing," *Wilson Library Bulletin* 60 (December 1985): 15–18.

9

Public Librarianship as an Interest Group

In his study of intergovernmental relations, Deil Wright has called the federal grant-in-aid to libraries "perhaps the textbook case of a single specialized programmatic interest group successfully achieving sustained national support."[1] The success of the library interest group brings out the fact that a small, well-educated, and politically aware segment of the population, even with a limited budget and affording one competent spokesman in a Washington office can, drawing on its national resources, organize its politically effective members into significant campaigns.[2]

In the play "Libraries Get Federal Aid," the name at the top of the marquee should be the American Library Association. That is, the chief credit or the blame (depending on your point of view) for the establishment of a federal role in libraries lies with ALA. . . . It was the ALA that first conceived of the idea of federal aid and it was ALA that was the initiator at almost every step of the way. Not only was ALA the consistent advocate but it was a skillful one was well. . . . The American Library Association did not wage its campaign alone. Fully aware that its clout in Washington was minimal, ALA from the beginning aligned itself with other interest groups to increase its influence.[3]

The centrality and significance of the ALA role cannot be overstated. Even if the ALA had been only half as influential as indicated by the excerpt from a study of federal involvement in libraries prepared by the Advisory Commission on Intergovernmental Relations, the results would still say a great deal about the importance of professional associations in U.S. politics.[4]

An interest group is an organized body of individuals who share some goal and who try to influence public policy.[5] This definition emphasizes the fact that the interest group must be an organized group, because it is the organizational resources that can be converted into political power.[6] An interest group is a political organization, since it attempts to obtain public policies that are favorable to its membership. The government is the target for the efforts of the interest group because only the government has the necessary powers and resources to satisfy the group's aims.[7]

To understand the *political* impact of groups, one must further distinguish between the overall group and its operations or involvement in Washington (or in state capitals).... Evaluating the role or impact of groups in the American political process is no easy task. Even after categorizing a group according to its goals, membership, resources, and activities, one must distinguish the overall group from its official leadership, evaluate both its Washington behavior and its grass-roots activities, and allow for internal schisms.[8]

Lobbying the nation's political institutions is only one of the activities of an interest group. The group also provides those who join it, those who pay its membership dues, and those who spend some of their time and energy on its activities with other benefits, which these members can enjoy.

Of the several groups active on the national level in matters relating to public librarianship, the American Library Association (ALA) is the most important. The stated goal of the ALA is "the promotion of libraries and librarianship to assure the delivery of user-oriented library information service to all."[9] The activities of the ALA are varied and include: research on library problems, development of standards and guidelines, accreditation of library education programs, support for intellectual freedom, publishing, continuing education, and lobbying on issues of importance to libraries and the library profession. In order to achieve these goals, some political activity is necessary.

The most important characteristic of the ALA is its membership. In its Internal Revenue Service category, the ALA is considered an educational, not a professional association. Unlike other professional associations, ALA membership is not restricted to professional librarians, but is also open to laypersons, as well as to libraries. Whatever its legal status, the ALA is perceived by librarians and by the public as a professional association.

Recruiting and maintaining this membership is, therefore, the association's primary task. Librarians join and maintain membership in the ALA for a variety of reasons, but there are certain incentives that attract and keep the members. The incentives to join the association are based on several types of benefits provided by group membership. The continued supply of these benefits will keep the membership stable. Material incentives are those related to tangible rewards that have a monetary value, including salaries and fringe benefits. Solidary incentives are intangible rewards obtained from the socialization and friendships that grow out of group interaction and the prestige associated with the group. Purposive incentives are intangible rewards that individual members receive from the satisfaction of being part of a worthwhile association.[10] The ALA carries out symbolic functions for its members that underscore their self-identification as librarians.

The ALA provides some economic functions to its members and information functions to both its members and the general public. Indeed, the distribution of information is one of the major functions of professional associations such as the ALA.

Professional associations are oligarchic, but there are certain democratic procedures that give legitimacy to the association. The membership, however, has little direct influence on the organization's leaders and on the formulation of the leadership's policies.[11] Although the members elect the leadership of the ALA, they do not really control their leaders. They do, however, have some chance to communicate their sentiments in conventions and through other outlets. Members may try to influence the policies and decisions of the association through conventions, which all members are free to attend. They can also express themselves directly by ballot and polls. Conventions, however, are controlled by the professional staff of the association. They are policy-ratifying, not policy-making, bodies, since the professional staff generally sets the agenda and prepares the resolutions. Conventions do, however, serve as restraints on policy makers and can moderate controversial resolutions.

Members exert some constraint and control over the organization's leadership by their potential for negative action. Members can leave the association with the nonrenewal of their membership. "Leaders are limited by the followers' expressed or latent values and expectations."[12] Membership meetings can be important on certain occasions, sometimes forcing the association to adopt policies not favored by its leadership or the professional staff.

The professional staff, which runs the association's headquarters and its Washington office on a day-to-day basis, is a dominant influence in the ALA as in all other interest groups. Although the governing body of the association has the responsibility for making organizational policy decisions, its decisions are often pro forma. The council will generally approve policies that have been initiated and determined by the professional staff. "In terms of deciding which issues to lobby on, allocating resources between advocacy efforts, formulating major aspects of strategies and tactics, and generally developing policy positions, the professional staffs tend to be the primary locus of influence."[13]

MEMBERSHIP CHARACTERISTICS

The size of the ALA is only marginally important. In 1984 it had some 40,000 members, of which some 3,000 were organizations, and the rest personal members. Not all professional librarians, however, are members of the ALA. In 1982 of 21,600 professional librarians working in American public libraries, only some 8,200 librarians were members of the ALA. Even if not all public librarians are members of the ALA, the association has a certain legitimacy. It does represent a significant segment of the library profession and can speak with considerable authority on matters of public librarianship. It can speak for the library profession in general; it has the ability to mobilize its membership strength for political action.

The membership of the American Library Trustee Association (ALTA) represents only a very small number of public library library board members. As policy makers, ALTA members are concerned with the provision of adequate financing for libraries and the passage of suitable legislation. In practice, ALTA defines its role and responsibilities narrowly and leaves the responsibility for professional action to other divisions of the ALA.[14]

Geographical dispersion is more important to an interest group than numerical size. "If one wants to get something from the whole House membership, it is important to have group members in a large number of congressional districts. The interest group that is widely dispersed is in a position to appeal directly to a large share of the House membership from their constituencies."[15]

The professional associations also act as an arm of the states by mobilizing expertise and political muscle, because "associations ostensibly composed of professionals in their private capacities, such as the American Library Association...often represent state agency interests."[16]

INTEREST GROUP COHESION

Another important resource is membership cohesion. David Truman has observed that the problem of cohesion was a critical one, and that the degree of unity in a group was probably the most fundamental in determining the measure of success it will enjoy.[17] While the ALA represents those who operate public libraries, it also represents some of those who use public libraries. Political participants on the federal and state arenas must feel that the group lobbying them is representative of group membership opinions. When a group is unwilling or unable to speak with one voice, political actors will refuse to make policy on the subject under controversy. "Without at least a modicum of unanimity, a group finds itself unable to take a position and base legislative action on it."[18] This point was stressed by Congressman William D. Ford, chairman of the House Subcommittee on Postsecondary Education, in regard to the proposal to establish a national periodicals center:

I have not, at any time during the years that we have had this before the committee, been able to perceive that the library community— the professionals who are frequently talking to us—has spent much time trying to get on one side or the other of the issue. It looks like it is the kind of thing where it is more comfortable not to take sides. . . . Frankly, you cannot tell from our record where you folks are.[19]

While the ALA is not completely free from internal conflicts concerning policy decisions, the association will try to avoid controversy and to adopt policies or lobby on issues, that will not split the membership. Taking a position on any controversial issue that may risk substantial dissatisfaction among various segments of the membership will be avoided by the association, although this has not always been possible, particularly in regard to social issues. For example, since more than one-third of ALA members are in management positions,[20] and since some 5 percent of the membership are members of public library boards, the ALA rejected the role of a collective bargaining agent for professional librarians in order to retain library administrators and library trustees in the association, as well as its tax-exempt status. The ALA still maintains that professional librarians and administrators can work out their problems within one association. "They say that a showing of unity is essential if the profession as a whole is to advance in competition with other professions and groups for public favor and public funds."[21]

FUNDS

While money is considered the most important resource available to groups in influencing public policy, library groups seldom use it, because substantial financial resources are not available to them. Financed largely from membership dues, library interest groups do not have the financial resources to give campaign contributions. The library interest groups do not have political action committees (PACs), nor do they play an open role in elections or endorse candidates for public office.

INFORMATION

The ability of a group to command facts, figures, and technical information in support of its position is another key organizational resource. Again, the group must speak to legislators and to bureaucrats without having any major internal disagreement. "Experts are aware that they cannot disagree among themselves if they want the prince and others to listen."[22]

ACCESS TO DECISION MAKERS

Access to decision makers is an essential commodity for the interest group, so that it may express its views on any proposal of concern to it. "Access to political decisionmakers is the key to group activity, and the nature of that access—the number of points of access, the ability to reach the 'right' people, the type of reception from the decisionmakers—is directly related to the resources of the group and its ability to utilize them."[23] The fact that there are librarians and library board members in every congressional district has been very useful in obtaining access to legislators.

LIBRARY LOBBY

Lobbying activities are only a small, but a very significant, part of the activities of the ALA. The lobbying potential of the ALA is determined largely by its characteristics and resources, which assist it in its pursuit of influence and political power. The ALA's federal legislative program is "based on an officially adopted legislative policy and a flexible legislative strategy."[24] The federal legislative policy of the ALA is formally prepared and updated periodically by the ALA Legislation Committee and adopted by the ALA council, for the guidance of the ALA lobbying activities. These activities are conducted mainly by the ALA Washington Office. The director of the ALA Washington Office is the main library lobbyist, indeed the only registered library lobbyist.

As far as public librarianship is directly concerned, the objectives of ALA's legislative policy are two: (1) the primary and most important objective is increased federal funding; (2) the second objective is the participation of the public library in legislation designed to create or strengthen community services and programs.[25]

Like other interest groups, library interest groups want to obtain from the federal government: (1) protection from harm, (2) favorable rules and resources, and (3) respectability and recognition.[26] The ALA Washington office monitors governmental activities that might affect libraries and the library profession. Many federal laws and regulations may wittingly or unwittingly, directly or indirectly, cause some kind of harm to libraries or to the library profession. The ALA lobby will oppose and try to block governmental activities or proposed governmental actions that would work to the detriment of libraries and the library profession, such as the revision of the classification and qualification standards for federal librarians proposed in 1981 by the Office of Personnel Management. It will encourage those governmental activities that benefit libraries and the library profession; it will initiate governmental action to promote their interests. It will promote the public library interest through the passage of new programs and the alteration, continuation, and increased funding of existing programs.

The functions of the ALA Washington Office are:

1. to provide the three branches of government with information about library services, resources, plans, requirements, construction, and labor;

2. to provide ALA members and state library associations with information on legislation and administrative proposals, plans, pol-

icies, and activities relating to the field at all levels of government; and

3. to provide liaison with other Washington-based representatives of appropriate groups.

An important concept used by the library lobby is its contention that the interests of the library profession and the public interest are identical, and that the library profession is always on the side of the public interest. The insistence that the library profession is speaking not just for itself but for all citizens is set out in the statement that "the library lobby is one of very few that takes as its constituents, not the narrowly focused demands of one special interest, but rather, the basic need of citizens for information to become economically independent, enhance the quality of life, and be sufficiently well informed to govern themselves."[27]

In their efforts to influence what goes on in government, interest groups in Washington use a variety of techniques. The most commonly used techniques of exercising influence are:

1. Testifying at hearings.
2. Contacting government officials directly.
3. Engaging in informal contacts with officials.
4. Presenting research results or technical information.
5. Sending letters to organization members to inform them about the group's activities.
6. Entering into coalitions with other organizations.
7. Attempting to shape the implementation of policies.
8. Talking with the press and the media.
9. Consulting with government officials to plan legislative strategy.
10. Helping to draft legislation.
11. Inspiring letter-writing or telegram campaigns.
12. Shaping the government's agenda by raising new issues and calling attention to previously ignored problems.
13. Mounting grass-roots lobbying efforts.
14. Having influential constituents contact their congressman's office.
15. Helping to draft regulations, rules, or guidelines.

16. Serving on advisory commissions and boards.

17. Alerting congressmen to the effects of a bill on their districts.

18. Filing suit or engaging in litigation.[28]

The ALA's lobbying activities are important to politicians, especially congressmen, because:

1. they can provide important information to support legislators' positions, or to help them make a policy decision;

2. they can assist legislators with political strategy, assist them in building a coalition, identify their allies, and coordinate the legislative effort;

3. they can provide legislators with ideas and innovative proposals; and

4. they can apply pressure to legislators in Congress and in their home district or state.

CULTIVATION OF GRASS ROOTS

Interest groups influence congressional behavior through the cultivation of grass-roots pressures. The importance of grass-roots efforts remains paramount. Congressmen say that unless the interest group has some connection with their constituencies, the group has little or no influence on their decisions. The constituency base makes it easier for the library interest group to get through to congressmen. The library interest group has this kind of an advantage because it has members in every congressional district and can appeal through them directly to all members of Congress. The ALA Washington office aims its grass-roots activities to the more active members of the association, those who can be mobilized, who are more likely to write letters to members of Congress, and who work to stimulate additional grass-roots activity. The Washington office communicates with the active members through *The ALA Washington Newsletter*. The ALA has also established a national legislative network and alerts its members to legislative developments, so they may keep the legislators and their aides informed.

COALITIONS

The library lobby has joined ad hoc coalitions with other groups having the same common concerns. Such coalitions are a very useful legislative technique and can exercise real influence on policy. "Coalitions not only concentrate effort and assure that like-minded organizations do not work at cross-purposes, they also increase the strength—or clout, if you will—of each organization that joins the common effort."[29]

RELATIONS WITH CONGRESS

Interest groups rank third in congressmen's decision making, after fellow congressmen and constituencies, but interest groups are only important in a quarter of the decisions. In 65 percent of congressmen's decision making, no interest groups or only one group are involved. Library issues decided by Congress seldom involve conflict between several opposing interest groups. Rather, the conflict to be decided by Congress is generally between the library interest group and the administration. Library issues are not considered "big" issues, because the saliency of the issue, measured in terms of interest group activity, is low.[30]

RELATIONS WITH THE EXECUTIVE BRANCH

The library lobby monitors and lobbies various levels of the federal bureaucracy in the same fashion that it monitors and pressures legislators and congressional committees.

Since location in the federal organization connotes power or status, the ALA and the library profession have tried to create in the Office of Education and later in the Department of Education a separate and distinct administrative office, such as an Office of Library and Information Services under an assistant secretary of education for library and information services.[31] Since the library profession wants to be seen and heard in the federal establishment, it has fought for additional visibility for the federal library agency and has tried to create, so far unsuccessfully, a federal agency that it could run.

Public librarianship institutions are the client of the federal library agency. Without these institutions, there would be no reason for the federal agency to exist. State library agencies, and, indirectly, public libraries are affected by the federal library agency and can exert influence on it. The federal library agency and the library interest group have an interdependent partnership. Federal library administrators and the library interest group not only coexist but also cooperate effectively and often. Federal bureaucrats need the support of the interest group before the appropriate congressional committees for maintaining and increasing their budgets and their autonomy in policy making. The political support and the information provided by the library lobby are important to federal administrators in defending their policies. As a result, the library lobby obtains access to and influence over one segment of the executive branch.[32]

RELATIONS WITH THE COURTS

The ALA does not initiate lawsuits in order to pursue its goals. It does, however, join the efforts of others to influence the courts by submitting *amicus curiae* briefs—formal legal arguments pertaining to pending cases.

Since the ALA is a tax-exempt organization, it is constrained by the Internal Revenue Code, which forbids it from devoting substantial amounts of its funds to lobbying. This fact has also been used by the ALA staff to prevent the organization from being involved in controversial political issues. One way to get around this constraint has been to establish an associated public foundation. To deal with issues of intellectual freedom, which often involved litigation, the ALA created a separate corporation, the Freedom to Read Foundation. This body, which was incorporated in 1969, helps to fund and to support lawsuits involving censorship and freedom of information.

SPECIALIZED LIBRARY INTEREST GROUPS

As the LSCA emerged from infancy stage, several new and specialized library interest groups appeared in the political arena. They assumed the traditional role of working to maintain the general trust and the basic structure of that program while seeking at the same time to modify it slightly in ways more responsive to their special concerns. These interest groups have offered modifications to the program that would more clearly benefit their constituencies.

Lobbying and influencing public policy were the major reasons for the establishment of Urban Libraries Council. This interest group is composed of about 150 large urban public libraries. The main thrust of the lobbying activities of the Urban Libraries Council has been to have the LSCA distributed to public libraries on a per capita basis and to obtain more direct federal funding for big city public libraries.[33] The Chief Officers of State Library Agencies (COSLA) was established in the early 1970s to gain more clout for the state library agencies and continued control by the states of federal grants-in-aid to public libraries.

Groups such as the Urban Libraries Council can weaken the library lobbying effort because they have certain demands that conflict with those of the ALA or the COSLA. The library lobby believes that in the long run "more is to be gained by compromise within a united front than by a more aggressive, more specialized appeal to the legislators."[34]

Crisis interest groups have been created as a reaction to the financial retrenchment of local governments during the 1970s. The National Citizens Emergency Committee to Save Our Public Libraries, a national citizen group, was established to seek more state and federal aid for public libraries. Other lay support groups grew out of the state preconferences which preceded the 1979 White House Conference on Library and Information Services. But most of these groups are concerned with advocacy and the creation of public awareness.[35]

CONCLUSION

Without having great political resources, the library lobby has been politically successful, appearing generally as a united front having a consensus and organizational talents in its lobbying activities. Librarians' effectiveness as lobbyists has been praised. One observer of the Washington lobbying scene reported that librarians "are alert, act on information they receive, and convey that information to their congressmen through the right channels."[36] But library lobbying power is limited and is felt only when it is concentrated on specific issues to which there is little opposition from other groups.

NOTES

1. Deil S. Wright, *Understanding Intergovernmental Relations*, 2d ed. (Monterey, Calif.: Brooks/Cole 1982), p. 227.

2. John M. Cohn, "The Impact of the Library Services and Construction Act on Library Development in New York State: A Study in Assessing the Effects of Federal Grants-in-Aid Legislation on the States." Ph.D. dissertation, New York University, 1974, p. 101.

3. Advisory Commission on Intergovernmental Relations, *The Federal Role in the Federal System: The Dynamics of Growth: Federal Involvement in Libraries* (Washington, D.C.: GPO, 1980), pp. 33–34.

4. Wright, *Understanding Intergovernmental Relations*, p. 228.

5. Jeffrey M. Berry, *The Interest Group Society* (Boston: Little, Brown, 1984), p. 5.

6. Ronald J. Hrebenar and Ruth K. Scott, *Interest Group Politics in America* (Englewood Cliffs, N.J.: Prentice-Hall, 1982), p. 15.

7. Dennis S. Ippolito and Thomas G. Walker, *Political Parties, Interest Groups, and Public Policy: Group Influence in American Politics* (Englewood Cliffs, N.J.: Prentice-Hall, 1980), p. 270.

8. Norman J. Ornstein and Shirley Elder, *Interest Groups, Lobbying and Policymaking* (Washington, D.C.: Congressional Quarterly Press, 1978), pp. 23, 26.

9. *The ALA Yearbook of Library and Information Services '85*, p. 44.

10. William P. Browne, "Benefits and Membership: A Reappraisal of Interest Group Activity," *Western Political Quarterly* 29 (June 1976): 261–263.

11. James Q. Wilson, *Political Organizations* (New York: Basic Books, 1973), pp. 237–238; David Truman, *The Governmental Process*, 2d ed. (New York: Knopf, 1971), p. 129.

12. B. Luttberg and Harmon Zeigler, "Attitude Consensus and Conflict in an Interest Group: An Assessment of Cohesion," *American Political Science Review* 60 (September 1966): 655.

13. Jeffrey M. Berry, *Lobbying for the People: The Political Behavior*

of Public Interest Groups (Princeton, N.J.: Princeton University Press, 1977), p. 196.

14. *ALA Handbook of Organization 1984/1985* (Chicago: ALA, 1984), p. 39; John T. Short, "ALTA Afloat in the Sargasso Sea," *Library Journal* 97 (June 1, 1972): 2054–2055.

15. John W. Kingdon, *Congressmen's Voting Decisions*, 2d ed. (New York: Harper & Row, 1981), pp. 152–153.

16. Daniel J. Elazar, *American Federalism: A View from the States*, 3d ed. (New York: Harper & Row, 1984), p. 183.

17. Truman, *The Governmental Process*, p. 167.

18. Kingdon, *Congressmen's Voting Decisions*, p. 169.

19. *White House Conference of Library and Information Services, 1979*, Joint Hearing before the Subcommitee on Education, Arts and Humanities of the Committee on Labor and Human Resources, Senate, and the Subcommittee on Postsecondary Education of the Committee on Education and Labor, House of Representatives, November 19, 1979. 96th Cong., 1st sess., pp. 53–54.

20. Leigh S. Estabrook and Kathleen M. Heim, "A Profile of ALA Personal Members," *American Libraries* 11 (December 1980): 656.

21. Corinne Lathrop Gilb, *Hidden Hierarchies: The Professions and Government* (New York: Harper & Row, 1966), p. 167.

22. Guy Benveniste, *The Politics of Expertise* (San Francisco: Boyd and Fraser, 1977), p. 24.

23. Ornstein and Elder, *Interest Groups, Lobbying and Policymaking*, p. 54.

24. Eileen D. Cooke, "The Role of ALA and Other Library Associations in the Promotion of Library Legislation," *Library Trends* 24 (July 1975): 137.

25. American Library Association, Legislation Committee, *Federal Legislative Policy of the American Library Association* (Chicago: ALA, 1979).

26. Stephen K. Bailey, *Education Interest Groups in the Nation's Capital* (Washington, D.C.: American Council on Education, 1975).

27. John Berry, "The Strength of the Library Lobby," *Library Journal* 110 (August 1985): 5; *ALA Yearbook, 1982*, p. 285.

28. Kay Lehman Schlozman and John T. Tierney, "More of the Same: Washington Pressure Group Activity in a Decade of Change," *The Journal of Politics* 45 (1983): 357.

29. Cooke, "The Role of the ALA," p. 141.

30. Kingdon, *Congressmen's Voting Decisions*, pp. 146–176.

31. White House Conference on Library and Information Services, 1979, *Summary* (Washington, D.C.: GPO, 1980), p. 52.

32. B. Guy Peters, "Insiders and Outsiders: The Politics of Pressure Group Influence on Bureaucracy," *Administration and Society* 9 (August 1977): 191–218.

33. *The ALA Year Book of Library and Information Services '84*, p. 286.

34. Art Plotink et al., "Washington Library Power: Who Has It, and How It Works for You," *American Libraries* 6 (December 1975): 650.

35. Barbara Cooper, "Trustees," *The ALA Year Book of Library and Information Services '85*, pp. 284–285.

36. The observer was Charles W. Lee, executive director of the Committee for Full Funding of Education Programs. Ibid., p. 648.

Conclusion

A major task for the politics of public librarianship is to analyze the various existing patterns of administrative and political control of public libraries and to explore the possibility of changing these patterns and devising new ones more suited to the needs of today and tomorrow. Certain future trends may have substantial impact on the public library and may require such changes. Some plausible future trends are:

1. More pronounced competition for financial resources on all levels of government.
2. Centralization and politicization of decision making about the public library.
3. Possible conflicts within the public library itself, between library administration and library staff.
4. Increased demands from the public for community participation in the control of the public library.

These trends will require library administrators to have more political savvy and sense, and to be able to mobilize the community for political action. Library boards, on both the local and state levels, if they continue to exist, will have to become more politically oriented and more representative of their communities. Library administrators will also have to share more decision making with the public. Most important, there must be more effective public library participation in the political process.

Bibliography

Abney, Gleen, and Thomas P. Lauth. "The Governor as Chief Administrator." *Public Administration Review* 43 (January/February 1983): 40–49.

Adrian, Charles R., and Charles Press. *Governing Urban America*, 5th ed. New York: McGraw-Hill, 1977.

Advisory Commission on Intergovernmental Relations. *Citizen Participation in the American Federal System*. Washington, D.C.: GPO, 1980.

————. *The Federal Role in the Federal System: The Dynamics of Growth: Federal Involvement in Libraries*. Washington, D.C.: GPO, 1980.

————. *Pragmatic Federalism: The Reassignment of Functional Responsibility*. Washington, D.C.: GPO, 1976.

————. *The Problem of Special Districts in American Government*. Washington, D.C.: GPO, 1964.

————. *Profile of County Government*. Washington, D.C.: GPO, 1972.

————. *State and Local Roles in the Federal System*. Washington, D.C.: GPO, 1982.

————. *Substate Regionalism and the Federal System: Vol. III, The Challenge of Local Governmental Reorganization*. Washington, D.C.: GPO, 1974.

————. *Substate Regionalism and the Federal System: Vol. IV, Governmental Functions and Processes, Local and Areawide*. Washington, D.C.: GPO, 1974.

Altman, Ellen, ed. *Local Public Library Administration.* 2d ed. Chicago: ALA, 1980.

Bailey, Stephen K. *Education Interest Groups in the Nation's Capital.* Washington, D.C.: American Council on Education, 1975.

Banfield, Edward, and James Q. Wilson. *City Politics.* New York: Vintage, 1963.

Berry, Jeffrey M. *The Interest Group Society.* Boston: Little, Brown, 1984.

————. *Lobbying for the People: The Political Behavior of Public Interest Groups.* Princeton, N.J.: Princeton University Press, 1977.

Beyle, Thad L., and Lynn R. Muchmore, eds. *Being Governor: The View from the Office.* Durham, N.C.: Duke Press Policy Studies, 1983.

Bollens, John C., and Henry J. Schmandt. *The Metropolis, Its People, Politics, and Economic Life,* 4th ed. New York: Harper & Row, 1982.

Boyd, William L. "The Public, the Professionals and Education Policy Making: Who Governs?" *Teachers College Record* 77 (May 1977): 539–577.

————. "Rethinking Educational Policy and Management: Political Science and Educational Administration in the 1980s." *American Journal of Education* 92 (November 1983): 1–29.

Brown, Lawrence D.; James W. Fossett; and Kenneth T. Palmer. *The Changing Politics of Federal Grants.* Washington, D.C.: Brookings Institution, 1984.

Browne, William P. "Benefits and Membership: A Reappraisal of Interest Group Activity." *Western Political Quarterly* 29 (June 1976): 258–273.

————. "Organizational Maintenance: The Internal Operation of Interest Groups." *Public Administration Review* 37 (January/February 1977): 48–57.

Bundy, Mary Lee, and Paul Wasserman. *The Public Library Administrator and His Situation.* Washington, D.C.: U.S. Office of Education, Bureau of Research, 1970.

Burlingame, Martin, and Terry G. Geske. "State Politics and Education: An Examination of Selected Multiple-State Case Studies." *Educational Administration Quarterly* 15 (Spring 1979): 51-75.

Campbell, Roald F., et al. *The Organization and Control of American Schools,* 5th ed. Columbus, Ohio: Charles E. Merrill, 1985.

————, and Tim L. Mazzoni, Jr. *State Policy Making for the Public Schools.* Berkeley, Calif.: McCutchan, 1976.

Christenson, James A., and Carolyn E. Sachs. "The Impact of Size of Government and Number of Administrative Units on the Quality of Community Services." *Administrative Science Quarterly* 25 (1980): 89–101.

Cigler, Allan J., and Burdett A. Loomis, eds. *Interest Group Politics.* Washington, D.C.: CQ Press, 1983.

Cistone, Peter J., ed. *Understanding School Boards: Problems and Prospects.* Lexington, Mass.: Lexington Books, 1975.

Cole, Richard L. *Citizen Participation and the Urban Policy Process.* Lexington, Mass.: Lexington Books, 1974.

Coleman, James S. *Community Conflict.* New York: Free Press, 1957.

Conant, Ralph W., and Kathleen Molz, eds. *The Metropolitan Library.* Cambridge, Mass.: MIT Press, 1972.

Cronin, Joseph. *The Control of Urban Schools.* New York: Praeger, 1973.

Davies, Don, and Ross Zerchykov. "Parents as an Interest Group." *Education and Urban Society* 13 (February 1981): 173–192.

DiLorenzo, Thomas J. "Special Districts and Local Public Services." *Public Finance Quarterly* 9 (July 1981): 353–367.

Downs, Anthony. *Inside Bureaucracy.* Boston: Little, Brown, 1967.

Dunscombe, Herbert S. *Modern County Government.* Washington, D.C.: National Association of Counties, 1977.

Elazar, Daniel J. *American Federalism: A View from the States,* 3d ed. New York: Harper & Row, 1984.

———. "The New Federalism: Can the States be Trusted?" *The Public Interest,* no. 35 (Spring 1974): 89–102

Eliot, Thomas H. "Toward an Understanding of Public School Politics." *American Political Science Review* 52 (December 1959): 1032–1051.

Ferman, Barbara. *Governing the Ungovernable City: Political Skill, Leadership, and the Modern Mayor.* Philadelphia: Temple University Press, 1985.

Finn, Chester E., Jr. *Education and the Presidency.* Lexington, Mass.: Lexington Books, 1977.

Florestano, Patricia S., and Vincent L. Marando. *The States and the Metropolis.* New York: Marcel Dekker, 1981.

Fox, Douglas M. *The Politics of City and State Bureaucracy.* Pacific Palisades, Calif.: Goodyear Publishing, 1974.

Garceau, Oliver. *The Public Library in the Political Process.* New York: Columbia University Press, 1949.

Garrison, Guy, ed. *Studies in Public Library Government, Organization and Support.* Washington, D.C.: U.S. Office of Education, Bureau of Research, 1969.

Glendening, Parris N., and Mavis M. Reeves. *Pragmatic Federalism: An Intergovernmental View of American Government*, 2d ed. Pacific Palisades, Calif.: Goodyear Publishing 1984.

Gove, Samuel K., and Frederick M. Wirt, eds. *Political Science and School Politics: The Princes and Pundits*. Lexington, Mass.: Lexington Books, 1976.

Gray, Virginia; Herbert Jacob; and Kenneth N. Vines, eds. *Politics in the American States: A Comparative Analysis*, 4th ed. Boston: Little, Brown, 1983.

Greenwald, Carol S. *Group Power: Lobbying and Public Policy*. New York: Praeger, 1977.

Hallman, Howard W. *Neighborhoods: Their Place in Urban Life*. Beverly Hills, Calif.: Sage, 1984.

———. *Small and Large Together: Governing the Metropolis*. Beverly Hills, Calif.: Sage, 1977.

Hamm, Keith E. "Patterns of Influence among Committees, Agencies, and Interest Groups." *Legislative Studies Quarterly* 8 (August 1983): 379–426.

Hamilton, Howard D., and Sylvan H. Cohen. *Policy Making by Plebiscite: School Referenda*. Lexington, Mass.: Lexington Books, 1974.

Hanus, Jerome J., ed. *The Nationalization of State Government*. Lexington, Mass.: Lexington Books, 1981.

Harrigan, John J. *Political Change in the Metropolis*, 3d ed. Boston: Little, Brown, 1985.

Hastings, Anne H., comp. *A Study of Politics and Education: A Bibliographic Guide to the Research Literature*. Eugene: University of Oregon, ERIC Clearinghouse on Educational Management, 1980. (Document ED 193 808).

Hawkins, Robert B., Jr. *Self Government by District: Myth and Reality*. Stanford, Calif.: Hoover Institution Press, 1976.

Hawley, Willis D. *Nonpartisan Elections and the Case for Party Politics*. New York: John Wiley, 1973.

Healey, James S. *John F. Fogarty: Political Leadership for Library Development*. Metuchen, N.J.: Scarecrow Press, 1974.

Heilig, Peggy, and Robert J. Mundt. *Your Voice at City Hall: The Politics, Procedures and Policies of District Representation*. Albany: State University of New York Press, 1984.

Hill, Richard Child. "Separate and Unequal: Governmental Inequality in the Metropolis." *American Political Science Review* 68 (December 1974): 1557–1568.

Hines, Edward R., and Leifs S. Hartmark. *Politics of Higher Education*. Washington, D.C.: American Association for Higher Education, 1980.

Holley, Edward G. and Robert F. Schremser. *The Library Services and Construction Act: An Historical Overview from the Viewpoint of Major Participants.* Greenwich, Conn.: JAI Press, 1983.

Hrebenar, Ronald J. and Ruth K. Scott, *Interest Group Politics in America.* Englewood Cliffs, N.J.: Prentice-Hall, 1982.

Iannaccone, Laurence. *Politics in Education.* New York: The Center for Applied Research in Education, 1967.

———, and Peter J. Cistone. *The Politics of Education.* Eugene, Ore.: University of Oregon, ERIC Clearinghouse on Educational Management, 1974.

Iannaccone, Laurence, amd Frank Lutz. *Politics, Power and Policy.* Columbus, Ohio: Charles E. Merrill, 1970.

Jennings, Robert E. "School Advisory Councils in America: Frustration and Failure," in *The Politics of School Government,* ed. George Baron. Oxford: Pergamon Press, 1981, pp. 23–51.

Jones, Bryan D. *Governing Buildings and Building Government: A New Perspective on the Old Party.* University, Al.: University of Alabama Press, 1985.

Josey, E. S., ed. *Libraries in the Political Process.* Pheonix, Ariz.: Oryx Press, 1980.

Kerr, Norman D. "The School Board as an Agency of Legitimization." *Sociology of Education* 38 (Autumn 1964): 34–59.

Kincaid, John, ed. *Political Culture, Public Policy and the American States.* Philadelphia: Institute for the Study of Human Issues, 1982.

Kirst, Michael W., ed. *The Politics of Education at the Local, State and Federal Levels.* Berkeley, Calif.: McCutchan, 1970.

———. *State, School, and Politics: Research Directions.* Lexington, Mass.: Lexington Books, 1972.

Koepp, Donald W. *Public Library Government: Seven Case Studies.* Berkeley: University of California Press, 1968.

Langton, Stuart, ed. *Citizen Participation in America: Essays on the State of the Art.* Lexington, Mass.: Lexington Books, 1978.

Levy, Frank S.; Arnold J. Meltsner; and Aaron Wildavsky. *Urban Outcomes: Schools, Streets and Libraries.* Berkeley, Calif.: University of California Press, 1974.

Lieberman, Ann, and Milbrey W. McLaughlin, eds. *Policy Making in Education.* Chicago: University of Chicago Press, 1982.

Lineberry, Robert L. *Equality and Urban Policy: The Distribution of Municipal Public Services.* Beverly Hills, Calif.: Sage, 1977.

Lockard, Duane. *The Politics of State and Local Government.* 3d ed. New York: Macmillan, 1983.

Lomer, Margaret, and Steve Rogers. *The Public Library and the Local*

Authority Organization and Management. Birmingham, England: University of Birmingham, Institute of Local Government
Studies, 1983.

Loveridge, Ronald O. *City Managers in Legislative Politics.* Indianapolis, Ind.: Bobbs-Merrill, 1971.

Lutz, Frank W., ed. *Public Participation in School Districts.* Lexington,
Mass.: Lexington Books, 1978.

————, and Laurence Iannaccone. *Understanding Educational Organizations: A Field Study Approach.* Columbus, Ohio: Charles
E. Merrill, 1969.

Marshall, John, ed. *Citizen Participation in Library Decision Making:
The Toronto Experience.* Metuchen, N.J.: Scarecrow Press,
1984.

Martin, David L. *Running City Hall: Municipal Administration in
America.* University: University of Alabama Press, 1982.

Martin, Roscoe C. *Government and the Suburban School.* Syracuse,
N.Y.: Syracuse University Press, 1962.

McGivney, Joseph H., and William Moynihan. "School and Community." *Teachers College Record* 74 (December 1972): 209–224.

Meier, Kenneth John, and J. R. Van Lohuizen. "Bureaus, Clients, and
Congress: The Impact of Interest Group Support on Budgeting."
Administration and Society 9 (February 1979): 447–466.

Miller, Gay J. *Cities by Contract: The Politics of Municipal Incorporation.* Cambridge, Mass.: MIT Press, 1981.

Mladenka, Kenneth. "Organizational Rules, Service Equality and Distributional Decision in Urban Politics." *Social Science Quarterly* 59 (June 1978): 192–201.

————. "The Urban Bureaucracy and the Chicago Political Control."
American Political Science Review 74 (December 1980): 991–
998.

Molz, R. Kathleen. *Federal Policy and Library Support.* Cambridge,
Mass.: MIT Press, 1976.

————. *National Planning for Library Service, 1935–1975.* Chicago:
ALA, 1984.

Nauratil, Marcia J. *Public Libraries and Nontraditional Clienteles:
The Politics of Special Services.* Westport, Conn.: Greenwood
Press, 1985.

Newberg, Norman A., and Richard H. De Lone. "The Bureaucratic
Milieu." *Education and Urban Society* 13 (August 1981): 445–
458.

Nielsen, Valerie, and Norman Robinson. "Partisan School Board Elections: New Evidence to Support the Case for Them." *Administrator's Notebook* 29, no. 3 (1980–1981): 1–4.

Ornstein, Norman, and Shirley Elder. *Interest Group, Lobbying and Policymaking.* Washington, D.C.: Congressional Quarterly Press, 1978.

Ostrom, Elinor. "Metropolitan Reform: Propositions Derived from Two Traditions." *Social Science Quarterly* 52 (December 1972): 474–493.

———. "Size and Performance in a Federal System." *Publius* 6 (Spring 1976): 33-73.

Paddison, Ronan. *The Fragmented State: The Political Geography of Power.* New York: St. Martin's Press, 1983.

Peterson, Paul E. "The Politics of American Education." *Review of Research in Education* 2 (1974): 348–389.

Piele, Philip K., and John S. Hall. *Budgets, Bonds, and Ballots.* Lexington, Mass.: Lexington Books, 1973.

Rehfuss, John. *Public Administration as Political Process.* New York: Charles Scribner's Sons, 1973.

Rich, Richard C., ed. *The Politics of Urban Public Services.* Lexington, Mass.: Lexington Books, 1982.

———, and Walter A. Rosenbaum, eds. "Citizen Participation in Public Policy." *Journal of Applied Behavioral Science* 17 (October–December 1981): 436–614.

Rich, Richard L. "Neglected Issues in the Study of Urban Service Distribution: A Research Agenda." *Urban Studies* 16 (June 1979): 143–156.

Robbins, Jane. *Citizen Participation and Public Library Policy.* Metuchen, N.J.: Scarecrow Press, 1975.

Rosenthal, Alan, ed. *Governing Education: A Reader on Politics, Power, and Public School Policy.* Garden City, N.Y.: Anchor Books, 1969.

———. *Legislative Life: People, Process, and Performance in the American States.* New York: Harper & Row, 1981.

———. *Pedagogues and Power.* Syracuse, N.Y.: Syracuse University Press, 1969.

Ross, Bernard H., and Murray S. Stedman, Jr. *Urban Politics,* 3d ed. Itasca, Ill.: F. E. Peacock, 1985.

Rourke, Francis E. *Bureaucracy, Politics, and Public Policy.* 3d ed. Boston: Little, Brown, 1984.

St. Angelo, Douglas, Annie Mary Hartsfield, and Harold Goldstein. *State Library Policy: Its Legislative and Environmental Contexts.* Chicago: ALA, 1971.

Salisbury, Robert H. *Citizen Participation in the Public Schools.* Lexington, Mass.: Lexington Books, 1980.

———. "Schools and Politics in the Big City." *Harvard Educational Review* 37 (1967): 408–424.

Savas, E. S. "On Equity in Providing Public Services." *Management Science* 24 (April 1978): 800–808.

Scribner, Jay D., ed. *The Politics of Education.* Chicago: University of Chicago Press, 1977.

Seidman, Harold. *Politics, Position, and Power: The Dynamics of Federal Organization,* 3d ed. New York: Oxford University Press, 1980.

Shavit, David. *Federal Aid and State Library Agencies: Federal Policy Implementation.* Westport, Conn.: Greenwood Press, 1985.

Shoham, Snunith. *Organizational Adaptation by Public Libraries.* Westport, Conn.: Greenwood Press, 1984.

Stetzer, Donald F. *Special Districts in Cook County: Toward a Geography of Local Government.* Chicago: University of Chicago, Department of Geography, 1975.

Stewart, William H., Jr. *Citizen Participation in Public Administration.* University: University of Alabama, Bureau of Public Administration, 1976.

Stroufe, Gerald E. "Interest Groups and Public Policy: A Status Report." *Education and Urban Society* 13 (February 1984): 149–171.

———. "State School Board Members and Educational Policy." *Administrator's Notebook* 19, no. 2 (October 1970): 1–4.

Summerfield, Harry L. *Power and Process: The Formulation and Limits of Federal Educational Policy.* Berkeley, Calif.: McCutchan, 1974.

Thomas, Norman C. *Education in National Politics.* New York: David McKay, 1975.

Thompson, John Thomas. *Policymaking in American Public Education.* Englewood Cliffs, N.J.: Prentice-Hall, 1976.

Timpane, Michael, ed. *The Federal Interest in Financing Schooling.* Cambridge, Mass.: Ballinger, 1978.

Trounstine, Philip J., and Terry Christensen. *Movers and Shakers: The Study of Community Power.* New York: St. Martin's Press, 1982.

Truman, David. *The Government Process: Political Interests and Public Opinion,* 2d ed. New York: Knopf, 1971.

Tucker, Harvey J., and L. Harmon Zeigler. *The Politics of Educational Governance: An Overview.* Eugene: University of Oregon, ERIC Clearinghouse on Educational Management, 1980.

———. *Professionals Versus the Public: Attitudes, Communication, and Response in School Districts.* New York: Longman, 1980.

Viteritti, Joseph P. *Across the River: Politics and Education in the City.* New York: Holmes & Meier, 1983.

Walker, David B. *Toward a Functioning Federalism.* Cambridge, Mass.: Winthrop, 1981.

Warren, Robert O. *Government in Metropolitan Regions: A Reappraisal of Fractionated Political Organization.* Davis: University of California, Institute of Governmental Affairs, 1966.

Wellisch, Jean, et al. *The Public Library and Federal Policy.* Westport, Conn.: Greenwood Press, 1974.

Williams, Mary Frase, ed. *Government in the Classroom: Dollars and Power in Education.* New York: Praeger, 1979.

Wilson, Graham K. *Interest Groups in the United States.* Oxford: Clarendon Press, 1981.

Wilson, James Q. *Political Organizations.* New York: Basic Books, 1973.

Wirt, Frederick M., ed. "Political Trends and Washington's Role in Education in the 1980s." *Teachers College Record* 84 (Spring 1983): 670-752.

———. *The Polity of the School: New Research in Educational Politics.* Lexington, Mass.: Lexington Books, 1975.

———, and Michael W. Kirst. *Schools in Conflict: The Politics of Education.* Berkeley, Calif.: McCutchan, 1982.

Wright, Deil S., *Understanding Intergovernmental Relations.* 2d ed. Monterey, Calif.: Brooks/Cole, 1982.

Zeigler, L. Harmon and M. Kent Jennings. *Governing American Schools: Political Interaction in Local School Districts.* North Scituate, Mass.: Duxbury Press, 1974.

———, Ellen Kehoe, and Jane Reisman. *City Managers and School Superintendents: Response to Community Conflict.* New York: Praeger, 1985.

Zimmerman, Joseph F. *State-Local Relations: A Partnership Approach.* New York: Praeger, 1983.

Index

About the Author

DAVID SHAVIT is Assistant Professor of Library Science, Northern Illinois University, at DeKalb. He is the author of *Federal Aid and State Library Agencies: Federal Policy Implementation* (Greenwood Press, 1985) and *Library Organization and Management: The Public Library*. His articles on library services and library history journals have been published in *Library Quarterly*, *Public Library Quarterly*, *Journal of Library History*, and *The Reference Librarian*.